Detox Christian Dating:

An Examination & Detoxification of Christian Dating Culture

By Landen Swain

Reviews for Detox Christian Dating

"What Swain presents here is a rarity in modern relationships, but ironically should be the standard." **-Cole Carpenter,** aspiring author of the upcoming book, *A Third and Holy Road*

"Detox Christian Dating takes an honest, vulnerable, deep dive into the complex web of navigating dating as a Christ-follower. Swain asks bold questions which require the reader to possess a genuine introspective perspective and willingness to obtain a wide-lens view of Christian dating. I was convicted in many regards throughout the book, and felt guided to work through those convictions by the discussion questions provided at the close of each chapter, and by Swain's commitment to include scripture and biblical truths. I urge believers who are single, dating, engaged, or married to read this book with an open mind." **-Hannah Altizer,** Blogger and Digital Creator for *The Honeysuckle Blog*

"This book is a must-read if you are serious about dating the biblical way. Landen's thoughtful approach to even the smallest details of the Christian dating culture earns this book a place on everyone's shelf. You will think deeper, wiser, and ultimately more biblical as you explore God's plan for your relationships." **-Kevin Wilson,** Host of the *Thinking Out Loud Podcast with Kevin And Kyle*

"Landen Swain asks the questions most Christians are scared to ask out loud… Swain does a great job of combining the humanness within us and the way we may all think sometimes and the grace and glory at the core of what God really wants for us.... Detox Christian Dating pushes us in a good way." **-Ben Lawrence,** Musician and Producer

"Christian dating is a complex topic that has seen its share of jokes and frustrations thrown its way. Landen breaks it down in such a practical way that is easy to digest, allowing scripture to bring light to an area that is all too often molded by emotion. A must read for anyone in the dating scene, or ministering to those who are." **-John Richardson (@JohnTheMessenger2.0),** Ruling Elder in the Presbyterian Church in America (PCA)

Copyright © 2021 by Landen Swain (submitted 9/28/21, filing pending)

Editor: Emlee Sanderford

Cover Design: Nanne" (99designs)

Swain Creations LLC (filed 2021)

Unless otherwise indicated, all Scripture quotations are from the ESV® Bible (The Holy Bible, English Standard Version®), copyright © 2001 by Crossway, a publishing ministry of Good News Publishers. Used by permission. All rights reserved.

Some quotes from the book were used by permission from the following:

Jesus, Continued…: Why the Spirit Inside You Is Better Than Jesus Beside You by J.D. Greear Copyright © 2014 by J.D. Greear. Used by permission of Zondervan. www.zondervan.com

Taken from *Holy Sexuality and the Gospel: sex, desire, and relationships shaped by God's grand story* by Christopher Yuan. Copyright © 2018 by Christopher Yuan. Used by permission of the author. www.waterbrookmultnomah.com

Charis: God's Scandalous Grace for Us © 2014 by Preston Sprinkle. Used by permission of David C Cook. May not be further reproduced. All rights reserved.

All other quotes were used by permission by the publisher or author, but copyright inclusion was not required or requested, but each source is properly cited in the Notes.

Table of Contents

A Quick Distinction: "Christian"	5
Introduction: Coffeehouse, John Oliver, & Surveys	7
Chapter 1: Should Christians Only Date Other Christians?	13
Chapter 2: Under Pressure	24
Chapter 3: Over Spiritualization	42
Chapter 4: Want a Word? Read the Word	56
Chapter 5: The Aesthetic Influence	69
Chapter 6: The Motivation Rarely Admitted	76
Chapter 7: Flexing Faith	88
Conclusion	100
Bonus: Miscellaneous Topics	102
Notes	121
Acknowledgements	129

A Quick Distinction: "Christian"

Like most southerners, I enjoy good chicken and hospitality. When I mention good service and food, a particular, closed on Sunday, fast-food chain comes to mind. What bothers me about them isn't the business itself, but how people talk about them. How they are deemed a "Christian" business.

Am I opposed to Christians? No; I am one. But where confusion sets in is that label of "Christian" being plastered onto a thing: Christian companies, Christian songs, Christian books. We use the adjective of Christian to indicate a certain content rating, the absence of sexual innuendos and profanity, or maybe even to describe the quality of something. But the question that intrigues me is how can those *things* be Christian? How can a song be redeemed by the blood of the Lamb? How can a business be justified by His grace? The lead singer of Switchfoot, Jon Foreman, had this to say about the "Christian" nature of the band's music:

> "...Does Lewis or Tolkien mention Christ in any of their fictional series? Are Bach's sonatas Christian? What is more Christ-like, feeding the poor, making furniture, cleaning bathrooms, or painting a sunset? There is a schism between the sacred and the secular in all of our modern minds. The view that a pastor is more "Christian" than a girls' volleyball coach is flawed and heretical. The stance that a worship leader is more spiritual than a janitor is condescending and flawed. These different callings and purposes further demonstrate God's sovereignty... None of these songs has been born again, and to that end there is no such thing as Christian music. No. Christ didn't come and die for my songs, he came for me."[1]

The title of Christian is most properly used to acknowledge a follower of Christ, not be the branding of an item or institution. As much as I try to avoid using Christian as an adjective due to the underlying incorrectness of the term, I recognize that much of the world has no ill-intent by calling things that cannot be Christian by that name. I'm not making signs and protesting businesses that are commonly described as being Christian, but I am at least mindful of the fact that a person can be a Christian but an idea, institution, or item cannot be.

As I discuss the subject of "Christian dating" I will occasionally refer to it as such with the common usage of the word "Christian" as an adjective in mind. As you enter into this discussion with me, I hope you will be thoughtful about how and when to use the word "Christian." I also ask while pursuing thoughtfulness we will give grace to those that innocently use it to passively refer to fast-food places and their favorite genre of music. Christ died for people, not things. Christians are redeemed by the blood of the Lamb, things will fade to dust.

Introduction: Coffeehouse, John Oliver, & Surveys

During my time in college, I got to host an event called Coffeehouse. It's essentially a themed variety show on a massive scale, with music and dance acts, games, student-made videos, and so much more all in front of seven or eight thousand people. As an appreciator of late-night television shows, I nearly fainted when my boss told me that the theme for one semester's Coffeehouse was "The Late Show." All my countless hours spent watching late-night entertainment would finally be put to good use. I was going to live out my childhood dream of being a late-night host. While writing the script, I imagined how funny it would be to see my professors belting a pop song during "Carpool Karaoke" or how a college dining hall is perfect for "Spill your guts or fill your guts."

After researching a wide variety of shows and their segments, I knew I wanted to do a variation of John Oliver's comedic research reports. For those who don't know, John Oliver hosts *Last Week Tonight with John Oliver* on HBO. His show digs deeper into everything from televangelists to professional wrestling and comedically exposes their more problematic tendencies. For the students of the Christian university I attended, there was one infamous thing that stood out as being notably overcomplicated — the dating culture.

Whenever the weekly chapel services at the university featured the topic of dating, the crowd was typically larger because many had been hurt by the dating culture, there's a bit of a cultural obsession with relationships, and despite the cultural fixation on relationships, many people do not know what to do once they are in them. Mixing people who don't know what they are doing with a dating culture that was more complex than the average community was asking for trouble.

I wanted to imitate the thorough research that John Oliver does, so I sent out a survey to gain first-hand knowledge of people's feelings on dating. As the results from the surveys came in, I became astonished at the overall sense of negativity surrounding the dating culture of my school. Yes, people did mention positive things and shared positive experiences, but a significant amount of people vocalized hurt, frustration, and concern. The word "toxic" was often used in the survey responses I sent out. Toxic is a bit of a strong word. Toxic has much more drastic implications in other contexts, and while I am not specifically using it myself, it is a word used often alongside a plethora of other adjectives to describe Christian dating culture. Therefore, I felt it fitting to address the alleged toxicity. Toxic means different things to different people but my understanding of the word is that it means that something makes life significantly harder for no good reason. When people say that Christian dating culture is toxic they are saying it is way too complicated, causes stress, and allows for problematic behavior.

It occurred to me that all of this may have been an isolated incident – it was entirely possible that the dating culture was just bad at my school and perfectly fine elsewhere. Mindful of that possibility, I reached out to several friends and even some strangers from all over the country to ask their opinions on the dating culture of their Christian school. This new survey pool made up of students from all over the country and a variety of denominations concluded the same thing and voiced the same problems. The dating culture was evidently toxic in places other than where I was. I even interviewed several students who were plugged into Christian communities at secular colleges, it became clear that there were issues there as well. Months into writing this book, a thread was started on social media where girls and a few guys told their "horror stories" of dating people from my school or dating Christians in general, which provided further evidence that we truly had a vast mess on our hands.[1]

As I was doing my initial research, I was ranting to my Dad about my findings and frustration. He confessed to me that all of the stuff I was frustrated about with dating cultures was present back when he was growing up. This wasn't just a modern problem; this was a problem that had been making romantic lives harder for generations. We had somehow allowed for toxic practices, policies, and tendencies to persist over numerous decades and seemingly not even address them, which was unacceptable in my eyes knowing that we as Christians can and should do better. We have a full-scale national, multi-generational, multi-denominational dating culture conundrum on our hands.

What troubled me the most was that it seemed like we accepted the frustrating complexity of it all. We had become complacent, adopting the toxicity as just some additional hurdles we had to jump over. Rampant bad theology being used to manipulate others, lovebirds boastfully making hasty decisions based on the wrong criteria, faith being used more as a flirtation tool rather than as something sacred - the more I looked, the more problematic practices and policies I saw. That is when a fire got lit within me to do the research on what the problems are, what makes them problematic, and how we can address the toxic practices and seek to adjust them for more positive usage or, if need be, eliminate them.

Think about dating cultures in terms of a truck: a truck has an engine, and that engine can be clogged up with all sorts of gunk that makes things more difficult. The truck can still get you to where you want to go but it would get you there a lot smoother if it did not have all of that gunk taking up space for healthy flow. This book seeks to act as an identifier of the gunk, explain how the buildup possibly happened, show why the gunk should not be there, and then provide a suggested solution to help unclog the relational passageways.

In terms of the truck analogy, it is clear that the solution is to unclog, but for the sake of not wanting to have this book be named "Unclog" which would likely result in it being confused for a plumbing manual, I decided to name this book "Detox Christian Dating: an Examination and Detoxification of Christian Dating Culture" because, per the title, we need to detoxify our dating culture. Considering the vast amounts of people that referred to Christian dating culture as being toxic, detoxifying it seemed like the appropriate aim. Some practices and policies might be rooted in good intentions but need a tune-up in some places to become less complicated and frustrating. We want to leave the dating cultures surrounding us less toxic than how we found them. I thoroughly believe that as a result of cultivating a better dating culture and by dating better we can reduce the divorce rate.

This book is not just for the young and dating. This book is also for leaders and elders of the church because the younger generation is a representation of what will become common within the Church's culture for years to come. The infection has already started to take place, but we can help to prevent the spread. Those who are older and maybe out of the dating scene should care about this topic because perhaps finding out what was unhealthy within your dating practices can help you to navigate through the toxic practices in your married life as well. For the sake of our present and future communities, we must work to identify problems and solutions for our dating culture sooner rather than later.

Let's Establish Some Things

"Yeah, I get what you are saying but I have this one friend who did that with his wife and they turned out fine." I imagine that as people read this I will receive a lot of messages like this one about outliers and special cases where a practice or mindset that I have identified as being toxic worked out for someone. The purpose of this book is to caution people in their approaches and ask them to thoughtfully consider their motivations and the actions that result from them. There will be some outliers that adopted a practice I identify as toxic that had it work out for them. A truck with a clogged-up motor can still get you to where you want to go but most people would love for the truck's motor to be without a lot of things clogging it up, making it harder to get where you want to go.

Additionally, I imagine that I will receive a lot of flak from people who say that who people date or how they date is none of my business. All I am doing is referencing scripture, trying to explain its implications, and stating observations that developed after hundreds of conversations with people frustrated by the Christian dating culture. If I notice something that is leading many to heartbreak and frustration and I say nothing, how am I being loving? I'll take the heat of being accused of poking my nose into other people's business for the sake of helping people avoid the same mistakes and heartbreaks that have afflicted me, my peers, and the generations before us. I want this book to spark honest conversations that can enable change and help us heal from our hurt.

When I say that something complicates the dating culture in a particular environment, I am not saying removing or detoxing a particular area of the dating culture will rid relationships of complexity. Relationships are complicated because two imperfect and complex people are trying to make a relationship work in an imperfect and complex world. What I am seeking to do in this book is address the overcomplication of something that is already complicated.

Aside from what scripture articulates as being a command, much of this book is guidance and advice rather than rules. For example, we will discuss making out later on and while it is not mentioned specifically in the Bible, I come to the educated conclusion that it is not wise to do so if you are not married and I highly advise against it. But I am not claiming that my advice and guidance hold the same weight as the Word of God although I will earnestly attempt to root myself in scripture.

I am not claiming that you have to hold all of the same convictions as me. I will stand by my educated opinions but do not demand that you adopt my view, but I do request that you approach these topics with an open mind. If you can hear out the reasons for why we should or should not do something, think through them, wrestle with your convictions, and come out on the other side still finding a particular policy or practice to be wise and beneficial, then I wish you the best and do not find you to be foolish. This book is my attempt at starting a conversation, laying my viewpoint and suggestions out in front of you, and asking you to consider it, mull it over, and then contribute to the conversation in nuanced discord, agreement, or further elaboration. I simply want to start hard conversations that beckon people to contemplate the outcome, motivations, and cultural contribution of their decisions.

Lastly, while I have done extensive cultural analysis and asked around about the cultures of Christian communities throughout the country, I cannot possibly be everywhere at once to gather the entirety of everyone's unique cultural experience. My observations may be different from your experience, and you are welcome to disagree on what is stressed or not stressed, idolized or not idolized, practiced or not practiced based on your experience. The observations I attest to here stem from surveying the general culture and getting feedback from people around the country. While you may not experience something that does not mean it isn't happening and just because I observe it that doesn't mean things are like what I have observed everywhere. We must each come into this conversation with that understanding and open ears to hear out each other's experiences.

Cards on the Table

I am not perfect in all of my dating practices currently or in the past. If you ever meet a person who handles dating and relationships perfectly, please tell them to contact me because I desperately need their advice. Mistakes have been made and through the process of writing this book I have uncovered things about how I would approach dating that I would consider toxic after careful contemplation. Calling others to pursue healthier practices and policies, I had to dive into deep introspection and reflection on the course of my life and realized that I have historically fallen short of some of the very things I call people to. In light of this, I am seeking to remove the logs from my eye, and encouraging people to reflect on the specks or logs they may have in theirs.

I'm not claiming to be the never-ending well of relationship wisdom, but I have put in the work to research these issues, hear people out, read books and articles, and ponder the solutions. I hope this book of conclusions I have conjured after extensive scholarship makes you truly assess your practices and motivations, brings about change if necessary, and inspires you to pursue healthier dating. But before we can dive into various aspects of Christian dating culture, a question about what to do about those who are not Christians in terms of dating needs to be addressed.

Discussion Questions

What has your experience with Christian dating culture been like?

On a scale of 1-10, with 10 being "Excellent," rate the Christian dating culture around you. Why did you rank the culture what you did?

In what ways, if any, do you think you contribute to the over-complexity of Christian dating culture?

Chapter 1: Should Christians Only Date Other Christians?

In the surveys that I put out during my initial research, some survey takers complained that they could not stand the exclusive nature of Christian dating culture that promotes only dating and marrying other Christians. While I understand where this complaint is coming from, the "cultural pressure" for Christians to only date other Christians is rooted in biblical wisdom and a long-term perspective.

A common thread throughout scripture is an appeal to marrying someone that holds the same faith as you. In Genesis 24, Abraham makes it abundantly clear how paramount it is that his servant finds a follower of the one true God as a wife for his son Isaac. For religious purity reasons, Deuteronomy 7:3-4 and Joshua 23:12-13 emphasize not marrying people of other nations because they would lead them away from following God and toward following the gods of their nation.[1] Proverbs 31:30 emphasizes how "a woman who fears the Lord is to be praised" and the typical commentary is that the type of woman that men should be looking for in romantic pursuit embodies that verse. 2 Corinthians 7:39 sees Paul instructing that widows in the church in Corinth are free to remarry, but they should remarry someone who is also a believer.

2 Corinthians 6:14 bluntly advises, "Do not be unequally yoked with unbelievers. For what partnership has righteousness with lawlessness? Or what fellowship has light with darkness?" While the passage's context is not specifically about marriage, the wisdom of that verse still very much applies and compliments what the rest of scripture has to say about who to marry. Think about it: who you marry is arguably (behind following Jesus) the most important decision a person can make, and God is supposed to be the cornerstone of your life as a believer. Far too often, we hear stories of believers who neglected the vast scriptural wisdom to only marry other believers, and then they live in a daily agony of knowing their spouse does not know the Savior they know. Raising children becomes a monsoon of conflict when one person is trying to raise their children in the ways the Bible instructs and the other is not. A believer and an unbeliever have two completely different value systems that are butting heads like rams. In compassion, I ask you this: is a marriage of

two individuals aimed at two very different points the type of marriage you want?

While scripture is clear that marrying an unbeliever as a believer would be incredibly unwise and discouraged, the Bible is less clear about dating unbelievers as a believer. After all, dating and marriage are completely different, and not all dating relationships lead to marriage. Dating is not mentioned in the Bible, as it is a modern invention. Abraham didn't take Sarah out for dinner and a show. Joseph didn't ask Mary out to coffee without clarifying what the intention behind the coffee was, and Mary didn't go running to Elizabeth to get advice on what Joseph could have meant by "we should go get coffee sometime."

The Bible sees single and married, not an in-between. Someone in a defined dating relationship with someone else is still technically single until they get married. Even engaged people are still single, although cultural traditions back in the context of the Bible would find engagement to be a much more significant commitment than our modern understanding. Singleness doesn't end until marriage begins. The method of evaluation has changed over the centuries, with each having pros and cons. But with dating being the modern fad, I think it would be best for us to learn how to do it wisely. It's simply another method of evaluation, and evaluation is biblical.

The logical progression of a dating relationship is that it will eventually lead to marriage. If you knew that marrying an unbeliever would be blatantly ignoring biblical wisdom and would likely lead to hardship, why would you even dip your toes in the water? I get strapped into roller coasters at amusement parks because I trust that they are certified by someone who knows what they are talking about. Why would I even strap myself into a roller coaster I knew was not safe or certified? That would be foolish. Why would I put effort into something romantically, financially, and emotionally that I know would be unwise to see go the distance? As a Christian, to date someone who is not a Christian would seem to be a waste of both your time and theirs if you are committed to being faithful to the teachings of God's Word.

Evangedating

Perhaps it stems from the years of watching courtroom dramas on television, but it seems like almost everyone is trained to look for loopholes in the system. "Evangedating" (also known as missional/missionary dating) is when a person uses dating as a tool to convert their significant other to Christianity. It is a loophole many try to use as an excuse for their unwise romantic pursuits of unbelievers. Admittedly, it has resulted in some genuine salvations. I know of several couples where a Christian began dating a non-Christian, and over time the non-Christian heard the Gospel and came to believe in the person, death, burial, and resurrection of Jesus. Praise God for it, but just because something happens a few times does not mean it should become the norm. For example, I got saved after cheating on a Spanish test and becoming convicted of my sin. Sure, God used my cheating to open my eyes, but that does not mean that we should go around telling students to cheat in hopes that they will end up repenting.

If you want a person to become a Christian, then share with them the Gospel. Faith comes by hearing.[2] Just sharing the Gospel with them instead of evangedating them could save you some nights out, maybe some money, and can even lead to a salvation. You may be interested in a relationship with them but point them to the ultimate relationship first and foremost.[3]

The fact of the matter is you cannot change a person. So many people get into relationships thinking that it is their mission to set a person right. To spare you a lot of confusion, frustration, and hurt down the road, you need to know that you cannot change a person's heart. Author and professor Heather Thompson Day's father once spoke into her life by telling her that she should never date a man for his potential.[4] She was advised to make her decisions based on who the guy is now, assuming nothing will change. The same advice goes for guys regarding girls. Potential means next to nothing if it never cultivates into something. Whether you are aiming at missional dating or looking to help a person along in their walk with Christ, you cannot rely on your influence to change a person's heart. You can't save anyone, and people are not projects.

An additional point of guidance would be that you should probably slow down when dating a recently converted Christian. This is not to say that this policy applies to all circumstances, but it is wise to mindfully consider their newness to faith and the maturity they may lack. For starters, you may want to see if they will take grace and their relationship with Christ seriously. In the exhilaration of the altar call, some will come forward to accept Jesus, but soon after leaving the gathering, they will unrepentantly resume the same lifestyle they were in, only this time with the misconception that they have a get out of jail free card in their back pocket thanks to Christ. You don't want to hop into a relationship with someone who matches the descriptions in Mark 4:3-7, where they wither away in their faith or yield no grain. You want to be in a relationship with someone who "...fell into good soil and produced grain, growing up and increasing and yielding thirtyfold and sixtyfold and a hundredfold."[5]

On top of that, we need to not settle for just Christian in name. Instead, we should be romantically pursuing people who are Christian in action. There are plenty of people who will broadcast their Christianity but treat you like they don't know God. Anyone can wear a cross necklace, lead a Bible study, go to a conference, do a devotional, attend a local body, have a Bible verse in their bio, and like worship music. But if you tore away the exterior aesthetic of Christianity, would you find faith underneath? Is there fruit evident in their life? By no means is someone going to be a perfect Christian, but if there is a blatant disregard for the Word of God and a lack of initiative in pursuing the things of God but all the boasting of being a Christian, then you are looking at an immature child (no matter their age) who you should avoid dating. They are probably not going to spur you on in your growth; they are likely just going to slow you down or redirect you.

"But I'm attracted to them, and they're a good person!"

People ignore scripture because of their comfort all the time, but especially when wanting to date an unbeliever because of attraction and morality. Scripture says beauty is vain and that God saved us out of His mercy, not by our good works.[6] They may be attractive. They may be lovely. They may be the cutest human being on the face of the planet with an easygoing family and a great career, but if they are not following Jesus Christ, then as a Christ-follower yourself, you need to steer clear of dating them because the things they have going for them are transient. Morality may keep them out of jail, but relying on their morality for salvation will keep them out of Heaven.

Undoubtedly, there will be Christians who do not listen to the wisdom of scripture and get into relationships with a person who is not a Christian. That may even be you. I know it has been me. If that occurs and you're dating or even engaged, I encourage you to have a hard conversation about faith and understand that even if it hurts or you have invested a significant amount of time into the relationship, a breakup between you two may be for the best in the long term. Or, if you have that hard conversation and it leads to a conversion to Christianity, you should navigate that relationship in light of this newfound faith. But it would be wise to keep in mind that some people will fake faith for a romantic relationship.

Some may think that breaking up with an unbeliever is unloving or has a "holier than thou" mentality. But faithfulness to God is not legalism; it's faithfulness. It's not "holier than thou," it's "holy is thy name." No one said being faithful to the Lord would be easy, but His ways are higher than ours, wiser than ours, better than ours.[7]

When it comes to an actual marriage where a believer is married to an unbeliever, Paul also speaks into that: "To the rest I say (I, not the Lord) that if any brother has a wife who is an unbeliever, and she consents to live with him, he should not divorce her. If any woman has a husband who is an unbeliever, and he consents to live with her, she should not divorce him."[8]

Paul's consensus is that if an unbeliever and a believer are married and the unbeliever wants to leave, it is permissible. This allowance furthers the argument that Christians are supposed to only marry other Christians. The hope is that the spouse who is not a Christian will come to know the Lord, but without a guarantee that they will, Paul advises the Christian not to get into a relationship with an unbeliever to start. As believers, we must value faith, develop it in ourselves, and then look for it in others when pursuing romantic relationships.

Hosea

The book of Hosea, known for being one of the boldest and beautiful pictures of God's grace, might be a point of confusion for many in terms of following scripture's standard of exclusively being in relationships with other believers. For that reason, an attempt at clarification is in order.

Hosea is a story in the Old Testament in which God commands the prophet Hosea to go "take to yourself a wife of whoredom and have children of whoredom, for the land commits great whoredom by forsaking the Lord."[9] Hosea then finds a prostitute named Gomer, marries her, and eventually, they have three kids. Numerous teachers observe that based on the wording of the text, only the first child is biologically Hosea's, further proving Gomer's infidelity.[10] It wasn't an "oh, she has a past, but now everything is fine" situation. This was a man told to marry someone who had sin in her headlights, not her rearview mirror.

Eventually, God instructs Hosea to go and buy his wife back after she runs back to prostituting herself as a symbol of restoration and love that God has for Israel: "Go again, love a woman who is loved by another man and is an adulteress, even as the Lord loves the children of Israel, though they turn to other gods..."[11] This is a picture of how God still seeks us even in our mess and the redemption that can take place because of God's grace and faithfulness to us despite our unfaithfulness to him, no matter what it is we have done.

At first glance, it appears as though God was giving open-borders permission to Hosea to marry someone living out a lifestyle in direct opposition to the Word of God. If God made that exception for Hosea, does that mean He is willing to continue making exceptions? Based on what we see in this story, is the policy of Christians only marrying other Christians a law or general guidance? We must remember that going on a date with someone, dating someone, and getting married to someone are entirely separate things. I don't think that getting a coffee cup with a person you discover to be an unbeliever is the end of the world, but continuing in the relationship and marrying them is unwise.

There are multiple interpretations of Hosea and Gomer's situation. Some find the story to be allegorical rather than literal.[12] The team of Ed Hindson and Gary Yates write another consideration: "It is not clear to some if Gomer was promiscuous before her marriage to Hosea or only engaged in immoral behavior after the marriage had occurred. Many interpreters have argued that Hosea retrospectively came to realize that the Lord had commanded him to marry an immoral woman after she was unfaithful to him in their marriage... If the command to marry Gomer was the symbolic act commencing Hosea's ministry, it would seem more likely that she was promiscuous when the prophet took her as his wife."[13] Regardless, their marriage was a symbolic act of our unfaithfulness to God but His steadfast faithfulness to us despite us and His grace to purchase us out of love. This speaks to our need for God, not His need for us, but clearly, He does want us. The book of Hosea communicates God's radical grace towards us. As Preston Sprinkle puts it, "Grace will not be a Christianese buzzword for Hosea."[14]

Through Hosea and Gomer's story, God is not communicating that we should do the same thing that Hosea did.[15] God often instructed prophets and others to do some rather unusual things in the name of symbolism – nakedness for three years, shaving one's entire head and beard, and even baking bread over dung[16] – but that does not mean that we should do these things too. I know I would be uncomfortable if someone informed me that my breadsticks were cooked over cow manure.

Some things in scripture are descriptive rather than prescriptive. In the story of Hosea, God was providing a beautiful picture of His love despite our sinfulness and unfaithfulness. Hosea is not a thumbs up on the decision to marry an active prostitute. Had Hosea disobeyed God's command to marry Gomer, Hosea would have been sinning against God, much like how Abraham would have been sinning had he not been obedient to God's command to sacrifice Isaac in Genesis 22. God makes the rules and sovereignly knows the implications of His commands.

All of this is not to say that non-Christians lack character or are undesirable. Gomer was made in the image of God and loved, even though God disapproves of her being a prostitute; there was always a seat at the table and love for Gomer even amid her prostitution. We cannot frame this conversation in a way that comes across as looking down on unsaved people as if they were somehow less valuable because they are not saved. Their value is present whether they are saved or not. Unsaved people are still very much made in the image of God, valuable, and loved.

A marriage between a Christian and a non-Christian can be a committed or loving marriage. Matrimony between two non-Christians can be classified as a good marriage. I am not trying to insult, insinuate a lesser status, or discredit the quality of marriages that have come about between two non-Christians or a Christian and non-Christian. But in a marriage between a Christian and non-Christian, only one of them is a part of a grander union. Scripture paints a wonderous picture of Christ being the groom and His Church being the bride, who are separated right now, with a responsibility of faithfulness to one another that Christ does to absolute perfection. But they will be united at the long-awaited wedding ceremony.[17] Christ sees the bride in all her imperfections but still loves her, died on a cross for her, and rose again to be with her. We are her. God met us in our mess and redeemed us.

You may never go on a date, get engaged, or get married, but those in Christ get to look forward to a much more significant, glorious, and eternal marriage: the marriage of Christ and His Bride, the Church. That grander marriage is offered only to those who are in Christ.

Am I What I Should Be Looking For?

Now that we have established the importance of Christians marrying within their faith let's discuss what makes someone a Christian. A Christian is someone who believes in the real Gospel. As a professed Christian who knows some of their Bible, you may understand that you are supposed to be looking for another Christian, but are you a Christian that a Christian should be seeking? Do you believe in the Christ-centered, grace-enriched Gospel and live a life that aims to reflect it? These aren't rhetorical questions. I want you to genuinely ask yourself these questions because many know all the terminology, have the right image, and are at the proper places but are entirely missing the cornerstone of it all: Jesus, His grace, His sacrifice on the Cross, and His resurrection. The Enemy would love for you to be deceived into thinking you believe in something you have never actually heard.

When assessing whether a person is a Christian, it is essential to not entirely rely on their claim to be a Christian. We do not know a person's heart, but we can watch for their fruit. Discuss their view of God, grace, sin, and the Cross. There may be disagreement on some theological topics such as Bible translations and alcohol consumption that are not deal-breakers, but a wrong theology on the core essentials (the atoning work of Christ, the resurrection, etc.) is a massive red flag.

This doesn't mean they have to have everything exactly right or know every bit of the Bible cover to cover (I certainly don't). Assessing should not feel like a theology exam, a spiritual performance test, or a robotic inspection; it should instead be a necessary but humble, grace-filled check-in on the core essentials to ensure they are present and authentic. Allow people to be flawed and human, for you are too, but hold to high and yet realistic standards.

We need to recognize that there are plenty of people in Christian communities who are not Christians because they do not believe in the real Gospel. Your reaction to that statement might be something along the lines of "he's crazy, look at all the people around me going on missions trips, working at camps, going to stadium-filling conferences, and listening to worship music non-stop. There's no way that they are not Christians." Brent Potter, a director for Kanakuk Kamps, which is an evangelism and discipleship camping ministry based out of Missouri, once shared with me that in his journeys across the country interviewing college students to work with Kanakuk for the summer, he has encountered plenty who cannot articulate the Gospel, plenty who believe a false Gospel, and plenty who have never heard the Gospel.

An abundant number of these are people who grew up going to church, have Bible verse tattoos, wear a cross necklace, attend massive conferences, have a Bible verse in their social media bio, and may even be a big fan of a worship band. One young man being interviewed described the Gospel as doing nice things for others to make the lives of others better. It had no mention of sin, Jesus, the

Cross, or the resurrection. Brent spelled out the full story of the Gospel for him, and the young man said he had never heard any of it before. That young man went to one of the largest Christian universities in the world. There are lost people everywhere, even in environments that claim to be "Christian," but don't be ignorant to the lost around you or ignorant to the fact that you may be among the lost. This reality check isn't fear-mongering; this is honest reflection.

What good is an earthly relationship with a man or woman if we don't have the ultimate relationship with Jesus Christ? We need to live for what lasts far beyond the grave. We need to live for the one who lavished and lavishes us with grace.

Our sin has separated us from God. We committed crimes against the King, and He has every right to carry out His judgment on us, the rebels. He must carry out wrathful justice on sin. Otherwise, He would not be just. But God, our King and Creator, loves His creation so much that He provided His Son to stand in our place and take the punishment we deserve. God's loving grace gave us Jesus, who we did not deserve and could not earn. Jesus lived a sinless life, died upon a cross, and then was raised to life again, conquering sin and death. The wrath of God was poured out on Jesus so that it would not need to be poured out on us.

All those who confess their sins, turn from them in repentance (not as works for salvation, but as a response from salvation), and follow Jesus as their Lord and Savior—believing in Him as the only one who could save—shall be saved. Die unto yourself, pick up your Cross, and follow Him. We are saved by grace through faith in Christ alone, unable to earn the righteousness of God through our morality or good works. Salvation is given as a free gift to all who believe in the righteous, risen Christ. This salvation is not simply a past event, but a present reality we live in that empowers us to live lives seeking to glorify Christ.

Salvation is not passed down genetically or secured through works, morality, or attendance. It is solely afforded to us by believing in the person and finished work of Jesus Christ, who stood in place of sinners by dying on the Cross for us and then was raised to life. Without the free gift of Christ, we are hopeless.

As you seek to find a Christian to start a romantic relationship with, be sure to prerequisite that search by evaluating whether you are a Christian yourself. There is room at the table for you if you are not. But even if we discover that someone is not a believer, we should not shun or shame them but instead lovingly come alongside them to point them to the most significant relationship they could ever know. The necessity of the Creator to creation relationship will always trump a creation to creation relationship.

Discussion Questions

For a Christian, how important is it to marry within the faith?

Is there anything wrong with evangedating? Why or why not?

Which should be looked for: a lot of potential or potential that has come or is coming into fruition?

Is it easy for someone to aesthetically be a Christian but actually not be a Christian? How so?

What is the overall point of the story of Hosea?

Can you articulate the Gospel?

Do you believe the Gospel? Are you a Christian? If not, what is keeping you from Christ?

Chapter 2: Under Pressure

The fear of missing out (FOMO) has resulted in many people doing reckless things. After two of my buddies started to make a little money on the stock market, I decided to invest a little myself to be in the know whenever they were talking about buying low and selling high. All that ended up happening was the line headed south, and my stress levels headed north. They just kept talking about the stock market, and I felt like I was lacking if I wasn't engaged in the trade. Those surrounding me were deeply involved in something that seemed to give them joy, and I felt as though I was behind in life because I was not participating.

Christian dating culture often feels like that. Everywhere you look, a couple is going on their first date, getting engaged, or getting married. Everyone seems so happy, like they are in on an inside joke. Social media certainly doesn't help you ignore it, and neither does almost every movie, play, television show, and song imaginable. Plenty of people advocate for singleness, and being a "strong, independent person" is something many desire to be, but contentment with being single becomes a lot harder when everyone around you is in on something you aren't. Of course, some of the discontentment is jealousy, but with the way that Christian dating culture elevates relationships and never ceases to revolve around them, can we blame people for becoming bitter over time?

The hyper fixation and overemphasis on marriage significantly contributes to the pressurized nature of Christian dating culture. Somehow the good gift to be held in honor (Heb. 13:4) has shifted into becoming the ultimate, a convention placed upon a pedestal as the standard of the ideal life. By no means should marriage be disrespected for it is a beautiful invention of our Creator, but when its influence results in everything being spousal prep, when all interactions must be viewed through the lens of romance, when singles are looked down on as late bloomers, and marriage is idolized, the good gift drowns instead of refreshes.

To further illustrate my point, I'll provide an example of what happened in one of my college classes. We'll call the professor Dr. Copper. I loved this professor. He was known for his hospitality towards students and had a reputation for being a bit of a jokester.

However, I don't believe he was joking when he told his class of impressionable young adults that we were making a huge mistake if we left the university we attended without being married, engaged, or at least knowing who we were going to marry. I get it; he's from a different generation that tended to get married at a younger age. And to his point, a college campus is a great place to meet somebody because there are typically many single people your age within a small radius. But telling a classroom full of students that we are fools if we don't have a wedding ceremony before or shortly after our graduation ceremony is just going to stress students out.

There is nothing wrong with a teacher or administrator encouraging students to date or even get engaged while still in college, but implying that they are behind if they don't find a spouse during their campus years complicates the dating culture. The primary goal of college is to get a college education, and if you happen to find someone to spend the rest of your life with along the way, then that is fantastic. However, to mandate that students find a spouse before going out into the real world or implying that there are not as many quality options outside of college is a pressure that should not be placed on students. A wedding certificate or engagement ring is not a graduation requirement.

Setting a timer on things pressures people to just want to get the job done and not worry about the details they need to consider. We as a culture need to steer away from a mentality that says if you're not married before the stroke of midnight, you'll suddenly become undesirable. We need to rethink how we talk about dating, making sure not to lift the gift of marriage onto a pedestal while stomping on singleness. We need to not treat having a spouse as being the peak of human existence, although it is a great thing. There will always be pressure in dating, but we need to take our foot off the accelerator by correcting our language, motivations, nuances, and focuses.

Four Pressures

I want to touch on four different common pressures I see within Christian dating culture. In some ways, these pressures overlap with secular dating culture but based on what Christians value, these things hold a little more weight in their eyes.

1. The Median Age of Marriage

When discussing relationships and dating, the statistic that people get married later than they used to often gets brought up. It is not that it isn't true, as the median age of marriage has risen over six years for both men and women compared to what it was in the 1970s,[1] but every time that statistic gets brought up, I wonder why it is a big deal. Whether intentional or not, constantly bringing up this statistic implies that those getting married later are somehow behind in life or making a mistake. Of course, the usage of this statistic itself is not troublesome, as it often comes with an elaboration on how we tend to date terribly, and that is why we take forever to tie the knot. But perhaps it just needs a clarification attached to it to clarify that we are not behind for not getting hitched by our early to mid-twenties.

I am not advocating that everybody has to wait for an extra half-decade before they tie the knot, nor am I saying that people need to hurry up and get hitched before graduating college. But there are a lot of things to consider with a decision of this magnitude. With all the implications of the marriage decision, maybe it is not the type of thing you should jump the gun on. Even though the endorphins that come with a new relationship feel good, things like financial stability and long-term integrity should be evaluated.

Don't let the fear of contributing to the growth of the national average force your hand into a hasty decision. If the delays you make in marrying someone increase the average age of marriage, so be it. The important thing is that you make a sober-minded decision that is clothed in prayer, informed by scripture, and inspected by wise, trusted counselors in your life.

2. Multiplication

We're so concerned with who is going to be walking down the aisle

when our primary concern should be who we are going to disciple.

The command to be fruitful and multiply[2] gets brought up in these sorts of arguments about when to get married, and for good reason. God commanded Adam and Eve to be fruitful and multiply in

Genesis. They were the first people and were to populate the planet. The Word of God offers a lot of guidance and encouragement about having and raising children and does not indicate that having children is a bad thing.[3] In fact, Psalm 127:3-5 proclaims, "Behold, children are a heritage from the Lord, the fruit of the womb a reward. Like arrows in the hand of a warrior are the children of one's youth. Blessed is the man who fills his quiver with them!" Since people want to be obedient to the command to be fruitful and multiply in the sense of family, they sometimes get eager to get married so they can get started on multiplying. It's a seemingly logical progression; the Word of God attests to sex being reserved for marriage. If couples want to be obedient to both waiting and multiplying, they should fast-track getting married.

But I fear that we have put too much emphasis on making kids and not enough emphasis on making disciples. Making children is something that not everyone can do. Men cannot birth children, and although most women have the capacity to, not every woman can medically, which is a common phenomenon to hear about in the Bible with the stories of Sarai, Hannah, and Elisabeth, among others. The Great Commission in Matthew 28:18-20 instructs us to "...go and make disciples of all nations, baptizing them in the name of the Father and of the Son and of the Holy Spirit, and teaching them to obey everything I have commanded you." Here, we see a commandment to teach others to obey everything Christ has commanded, whether that be our children in a family sense or our children in the faith.[4] There is a command to be fruitful and multiply, but in view of the entire Bible, it seems it is not exclusively talking about having kids; its implication is so much more. By looking at other parts of scripture, it would appear to include training up God-fearing disciples.

Those who are single currently or perhaps for their entire life do not have a marriage covenant to balance, which frees them up to make that much more of an effort towards discipleship. Paul noted in 1 Corinthians 7 his desire for people to remain single for that very reason. Even before Paul, we see John the Baptist living the single life and being faithful within it (granted, I don't know a lot of women who want to marry a man who wore camel's hair and whose diet consisted of honey and insects.) Both statuses are good, and both statuses are commissioned, each carrying unique pros, cons, and levels of responsibilities. Whether you are blessed with kids or not, be fruitful and multiply disciples. I want to be adamantly clear that this is not a deterrent from having children but rather a perspective shift on how we can all be parents, in a sense.

Emphasizing making disciples instead of just making children eases the pressure singles feel to get married, allows all to participate regardless of relationship or parenthood status, and focuses on what is biblically more critical. Those who do get married and have children will have more responsibilities they need to tend to. Parents are still commissioned to make disciples, but realistically, they have more to balance.

By emphasizing discipleship over marriage and parenthood, we become inclusive of the single or married and give a mission to all cognitive ages. But another group can monumentally benefit from the emphasis on discipleship over romantic relationships and childbearing. Based on some of the conversations I have had and the books I have read, those coming out of the LGBTQ+ community are often told that they now need to marry someone of the opposite sex, as if marriage is their ultimate purpose or will somehow "fix" them. Some possess or develop the ability to get into a relationship with someone of the opposite sex, despite the attraction they had or still have to those of the same sex. But for others, there is no romantic attraction to the opposite sex, so pressuring them into a romantic relationship with someone of the opposite sex does not seem practical or even healthy. But when our prioritization of discipleship is appropriately communicated, those coming out of LGBTQ+ relationships are included in the efforts of the Great Commission, rather than being burdened with the pressure of getting married to someone they may not even be attracted to. Every relationship status, sexuality, and just about every age can make spiritual children, but not all can make physical children.

To the currently childless and single, I say this: take in this time you are in, realize its vast value and potential. Then, make the most of it. You don't need to expedite processes and rush through life to try to be in the safe zone so you can start multiplying. Enjoy the present and take as much time as necessary. Multiply in whatever state you are in.

3. Biological Clock

Out of all of these pressures, this is the one I have seen played out the least, but I still want to address this minority issue since I have observed it. Realistically, it does become harder to have children as you age. After all, Zechariah recognized that his wife was advanced in years, and he was an old man, which would have made bearing a child virtually impossible, which is what makes the birth of John the Baptist so miraculous. The anxiety around having a "biological clock" holds the potential of women (and men) rushing through the evaluation process so that they can get straight to multiplying. Anxiety at the hands of fertility issues is an entirely valid concern, and I do not want to act like it isn't a big deal, but I want to gently bring up a perspective shift and silver lining.

Individuals often vocalize how they would love to have some time when it is just them and their spouse to settle for a few years and do things they know will become harder to do once they have children. Once you begin to do the math on how many kids you want, when you want to have them, added with the number of years you want alone and the time you have left until it becomes statistically harder to have children, it can become overwhelming. To some, the stress may lead to expediting the spouse finding process. When rushed, we tend to overlook things; searching for a spouse is not the type of process you want to overlook things in. I fear that some will get into a covenant with a person who would be terrible at raising kids just because they fear that if they don't before the typical ages where fertility begins to decline, they will miss out on the opportunity to have kids.

A few months after my high school graduation, I got to work at a camp in New York. Alongside other high schoolers and recent graduates from across the country, I served in the dining hall where we would serve tables, clean the dining hall, and set up the décor in between meals. Campers were outside enjoying games or inside the clubroom hearing about Jesus while we were balancing trying to get the dining room set up as fast as possible while also making it look as nice as we could. What would often happen was we would speed through the setup and then have to spend a significant amount of time perfecting the décor afterward. However, what seemed to work best was perfecting things as we went along. We knew we had a deadline but should not overlook what was important because we wanted to be done with the task.

The same goes for speeding through the evaluation of our potential spouses because we feel a monstrous pressure to get cracking on reproducing. Why rush and then have to correct for what you neglected when you could take your time and try to look out for problems as you go along? That's not to say the slowest and most patient pace will find you absent of problems, but you have a decent chance of avoiding some drastic issues.

Desiring children is not a bad thing; it is a blessed desire. But the desire to have children and marry a person of character should be equal. When a marriage is viewed solely as an avenue for having kids, the marriage may struggle or fall apart once the kids leave the house because no work was done to maintain and flourish the foundation. You're not just looking for someone to parent your child; you're looking for someone to be in a covenant with.

A good rule of thumb is to find someone you would want to raise your kids were you not able to. Evaluating if someone is the type of person to start a family with is not something to jump the gun on. Don't allow your fear of waiting too long make you slash your standards in half because you are fearful that if you wait too long, you will miss out on the chance to have children.

Parenthood has a myriad of blessings attached to it, but some people believe that only biological parenthood is good enough. Biological parenthood is not the only way to obtain the blessing of children. I hold the position, as do many others, that adoption or fostering care can be just as special as having a child biologically.[5] While you may have a rampant desire to "multiply" and hold a baby of your own (which is a good desire), you should not compromise your values to fulfill it. How about we reorient our view of adoption and foster care to see making disciples out of those who have already been born being just as special as having biological children and raising them to be faithful disciples? By not looking at foster care or adoption as "less than" options, we relieve ourselves of a lot of the biological clock stress because you can adopt and participate in foster care for much longer than you will be able to have kids. The icing on top of the cake is that by adopting, you are helping to meet the needs of our society, and you are getting to experience a beautiful picture of the Gospel.[6]

4. Alone

Among the first few pages of the Bible, we see a pattern of "God saw that it was good." Let there be light: good. The distinction between dry land and the seas: good. Sun, moon, and stars: good. But then suddenly we reach Genesis 2:18 where God says, "It is not good that the man should be alone; I will make him a helper fit for him." Adam, the man God had created from dust, was surrounded by animals, yet God recognized that this wasn't good enough for Adam. He needed a person to be with. Thus, Eve comes into the picture, the first acclamation of love is sung, and the first marriage takes place.

Fast forward to the New Testament, we see church planter extraordinaire Paul making the most of his singleness. Given God's statement, "It is not good that the man should be alone," it would seem as though Paul is living the rebellious life against that command. Although it has never been said directly to me, it has sort of always been understood that the expectation is for everyone to get married someday. We will often say things like "I can't wait to do that with my future wife" and ask hypotheticals about relationships, seemingly concluding that everything in our lives is preparing us for life with a spouse. But Paul lives in contrast to that conclusion, even conceding that he wishes others were as he is. In the context of that 1 Corinthians 7 passage, we can conclude that he was talking about wishing that others were single and content.

But the reigning truth is still that it is not good for man to be alone. So how is Paul living in correlation to that passage if he is single? How was John the Baptist or even Jesus living obediently if they were alone in the sense of marriage? If you've read Paul's letters in the New Testament, you likely have noticed the random shout-outs at the end of his writings to Pudens, Rufus, Gaius, Nympha, and others.[7] What this tells us, among other things, is that Paul was surrounded by community. He worked with people. He got poured into and poured out to others. He had a great love for his brothers and sisters in Christ and often found comfort in being around those he cherished. So Paul was not alone, which lives in correspondence with God's anti-solo act statement in Genesis.

Whether married or not, we were meant to live amongst others. We need wise counsel. We need people to pour into us and people to pour into. We need people to serve and have fun with. Although Paul had no wife to go home to, he had friends to surround himself with. Paul may not have had children, but he surely raised children in the faith. The pressure that tells us that we need someone is half true. Aside from our obvious need for Christ, we do need someone, but it does not have to be a spouse. We need community. As believers, we need people who will point us to Jesus and encourage us to follow Him. Where else are we going to find such a community other than the Church? We need to be immersed in a local body of believers. There are times for solitude, but we should not be alone. We do not necessarily need a spouse, but we need community.

Arrived

The elevation and idolization of marriage within Christian dating culture have conditioned us to believe that those in a relationship have reached some elitist status. It's as if everything in life has been leading up to the wedding, where all of the character and skill development is finally paying off because it has been proven to God that we are now worthy of a spouse. The phenomenon reminds me of that scene from Disney Pixar's Toy Story where one of the squishy toy aliens is selected by "The Claw" and is pleased because they have been chosen, proving their worthiness. Many a sorrowful prayer warrior has pleaded their frustration to God over not feeling like they have arrived at being worthy of a spouse when they have been doing all of the things that the culture has been telling them they must do and become what the culture says they must become. Whether it be feigning contentment or "walking in the spirit of a wife, not a girlfriend," so many singles are left hurting and confused because they are doing all the right things, and yet the thing society has been told is most important never comes into view.

By making it seem like someone's "time has come" and they have finally been deemed worthy enough to be chosen for a relationship, we manufacture a cultural pressure to be in a relationship and place romance on an even higher pedestal. Everyone wants to feel like they have gotten to the place everyone else dreams of being. We all want to belong and feel like it is our turn to walk in the sun. Christian culture has promoted relationships like it's the most brilliant inside joke. Singles have often been made to feel isolated and looked down on for not understanding what's so funny.

God does not owe us anything for our development of skills or characteristics. We have derived the "if you build it, they will come" philosophy from Disney's Field of Dreams and have tricked ourselves into a sense of entitlement. Yes, most people get married at some point in their lives, but just because we have developed practices and qualities in ourselves that would be considered spousal material, that does not mean that we will be granted marriage, nor does it mean we are entitled to it.

My hunch is that the "always the bridesmaid, never the bride" feeling our culture eggs on would diminish in power if we did not put relationships up on a mountaintop and act as if the ultimate climax of human existence is marriage. That's not to act as if a wedding or relationship cannot be a highlight or even one of our core memories, because surely marriage is something to rejoice in. If you're not excited about a relationship, then something is off-kilter because relationships are worth celebrating. The magnitude of the moment should be recognized. We should honor the great covenant that marriage is, but we should not idolize it to a point where we preach marriage over discipleship or act as if those who did not get married missed out on what life is all about. I often wonder if the broadcasting of our relationships on social media, the flaunting of our engagement rings and wedding days, our highlighting of the romance in our lives is because of the cultural status associated with being in a relationship. It's almost as if instead of knowing that we are loved, we feel a need to publicize and try to convince others that we are loved. Culture at large has convinced us that we are only truly happy, loved, or content if we can aesthetically prove it. Again, there's nothing wrong with celebrating a marriage, engagement, or relationship, but there is something to be said for the cultural clout that comes with advancing in a relationship.

You likely know, or maybe you are, someone who has to always be in a relationship and connects their worth with whether someone is pursuing them romantically or not. Perhaps you feel that if no one is picking you off the shelf, per se, then you really must not be that valuable. Based on real-life and social media observation, everyone around you seems to be in relationships, so you seem like the outlier because you are not in one. I have struggled with this, and I know many others who do as well.

In social media captions, song lyrics, and at weddings, we often hear the expression *my other half,* which has a romantic ring to it. One of those necklaces of half of a heart with a perfect matching counterpart belonging to the one we love most probably comes to mind. It's romantic but misguided at the same time. The thing is that you as an individual are complete. There is a hole in your soul that Christ can only fill; with Him, you lack nothing. Plain and simple, you do not need a solely human person to complete you. You are not missing a half. "He who finds a wife finds a good thing," but he who finds a wife does not find the ultimate thing in which he should find his worth. Marriage is not the pinnacle of joy, but neither is unashamed and unbothered singleness; ultimately, the presence of the Lord is where joy is found, not the presence of a spouse.[8]

Hear me loud and clear: I am in no way, shape, or form trying to disrespect marriage, as I hold it in nothing but honor. But I have felt and seen the isolation that has come at the hands of marriage idolization. And for that reason, I lovingly bring up this concern and encourage Christian culture to reorient how we speak about relationship statuses for the sake of avoiding idolization and point singles and those in relationships towards their proper fixation.

Loved Before A Spouse

People are often scared to break up with someone because that means abandoning their plans with that person for the future. But sometimes, breaking up is necessary, and that's okay. Not every relationship or date has to be a success. Not every date has to lead to marriage. Our tendency to shackle our worth to our relationship status has made breaking up so much more complicated or sometimes not even an option in our minds because we can't wrap our heads around letting go of what we have defined ourselves by for so long. We may have been somebody's someone, but in Christ, we are ~~sons and~~ daughters of the King, a status that does not change even when your dating status does. We want to find love, but love has already found us. We need to define ourselves by the unwavering, deeper-level love of God, who was faithful to us at high personal cost despite our insistence on finding our worth in things outside of Him.

If I am blessed with a wife someday, I know I am already blessed because God in His sovereignty and holiness still thought to save us. On the other hand, if I remain single for the rest of my days, I know that my life is not incomplete, and a wife will not complete it. Even writing this, I questioned myself, but while the scriptural truth is hard to follow, it is still true. Both the person blessed with singleness and the person blessed with marriage is just that: blessed. Each is given a unique life that presents unique challenges, lessons, and triumphs. We will likely find ourselves wondering what life is like in another's shoes, but we should not neglect to lace up the shoes on our own feet and serve faithfully where we are.

Ring By Spring

If you are around Christian dating culture, you almost certainly have at least heard of ring by spring. For those who don't know, ring by spring (RBS) is a multi-faceted term that refers to people getting engaged before the final semester of their senior year. However, it can also refer to underclassmen engagements. The phrase also encapsulates how many people seem to get engaged during the same part of the year. In essence, it's getting engaged young and often relatively quickly. In some conversations with people unfamiliar with Christian culture, they find it hard to believe that ring by spring truly exists. At some Christian schools, jewelry stores will take up ads such as "Looking For a Ring for Ring By Spring?" because they know that many students are interested in it. Nothing quite like adding an engagement ring expense on top of all that student loan debt. So yes, it is very much real, and you don't realize just how popular the cultural phenomenon is until you get into the dating culture.

Typically, people understand that those who have dated throughout college may want to get married shortly after graduating, and while people still joke about RBS, most of those marriages between young people are celebrated. Where the general cynicism and concern surrounding ring by spring comes is around the practice of rushed engagements, where it seems like two people who don't know each other very well wanted to beat a deadline. The concern is that people are making a lifelong commitment to someone that they may not know very well because they were only together for a short, "puppy-love" time period before deciding to spend their lives together.

The countless number of students seen getting engaged so suddenly instills an unintended pressure within the culture to be in a relationship and find someone to marry. As a result, it is easy to feel like you are behind in life if you are not engaged by the time you graduate. On a personal note, I felt like something was deeply wrong with me because I was not in a relationship by my senior year. While many things are likely to blame for that insecure feeling, including comparison and individual insecurity, the cultural pressure of finding a spouse before you graduate rightfully should take a share of the blame. In a later chapter, we will address the complex topic of sex being a possible motivator behind ring by spring engagements, but for now, we will discuss ring by spring in general. While I have already mentioned the cultural pressure aspect of ring by spring, I want to talk about the decision-making process and the outsider perspective.

If you tried looking for a verse in the Bible that tells you the exact amount of time you should date before getting engaged, you wouldn't find it spelled out for you. In truth, there is no definitive answer to how long you should take before engagement, and it will be different for every couple. I know people who just turned nineteen that have the maturity of a thirty-year-old and could make a wise decision regarding marriage. On the other hand, I also know thirty-year-olds who act like they're twelve and make terrible judgment calls. Your age (post-turning a legal age) is not the ultimate determiner of whether you're "ready" for marriage or not. Neither is your dating timeline.

A few questions spring up regarding engagement regardless of the relationship length: why do you want to get engaged when you do? Have you talked about finances? Do you want to spend the rest of your life with someone, putting them before yourself, looking to see them thrive? Do you want to be committed to someone for as long as you both shall live? Do you want to stand side by side with someone through it all, the ups and downs, the highlight reel and the bloopers, in commitment to never leaving their side? If the physical attractiveness they currently possess were to subside for some reason, would you stay committed to them? If the physical side of marriage could never happen again, would you still want this person and be willing to be faithful? These are some of the questions that must be considered when assessing why you want to marry someone.[9]

Alongside the reason behind wanting to date, get engaged, and get married, there is the concept of the weight of til death do us part. Genesis 2 tells us that two shall become one flesh, with scripture citing numerous times not to separate what God has brought together. That means the person whose hands you hold as you stand across from them on your wedding day will be the same face you will come home to every day. You will witness all their flaws, and they will see yours. Despite their faults and yours, you both committed to love each other and put each other first. Isn't a commitment that serious worth taking the time to patiently assess who you are entering into it with?

As wonderful as they are to be around, as good as they make you feel, take time to consider the fact that the excitement of a new relationship may cloud your judgment. The puppy love that comes with a new relationship or romantic interest may very well blind you to how they truly are. I'm not saying this to fearmonger or to make you build up a closed-off skepticism. I'm saying this to invite you into sober-minded discernment. Evaluate their character after you have been together for a while. Wait until the adrenaline has worn off so that you will be able to see them with their guard down.

Each situation is different. Some couples may have known each other for a long time before dating, so there is not an incredible amount to learn about each other before getting engaged. But keep in mind that engagement, dating, and friendship are all very different things with varying levels of complexity. The trouble with the policy of "let's get engaged first, and then we'll assess" is the financial and emotional investment already made by purchasing a ring. Breaking off an engagement is much harder than simply breaking up. The generally wise thing to do is to take your time to ponder what the seriousness of till death do us part and patiently assess the person you want to enter that sacred covenant with all while working on your character.

There is a preacher that I highly respect and listen to often who got married after knowing his now-wife for a little over six months. In hindsight, we see that they share a steadfast commitment. Their marriage has seen biological children and adoptions throughout its duration, and the risk that they took having only known each other for a little over half a year paid off. But here's the thing: it was still a risk. Just like how driving at high speeds gets you to your desired location faster, you also run a more considerable risk of getting into a wreck. What if one of them had been putting on a mask for a long time, only to reveal that they were a wolf in sheep's clothing? The patient assessment of character over time is the safer option, but it does not mean that the fast-paced approach is necessarily wrong. There is still risk in a relationship even if you know just about everything about them. This section isn't meant to convince you that you need a 100% money-back guarantee before committing to someone. Instead, it is intended to show that we need to be mindful that speeding into things does tend to cause more accidents.

Based on listening to this preacher for years and hearing how highly he speaks of his wife, I can rest assured that they were mature in their thinking. And while this speaker admitted to a desire for sex being part of the equation, he also was evidently mature enough to assess her character. He saw things in her that he did not even know he wanted in a person. Even if this speaker hadn't been mature in his assessment, once he got into the marriage, he committed to be faithful within it. Once you build your house, live in it.

The desire for a spouse is very natural but not required. You should get married because you long to be linked in covenantal commitment to another person. I recognize that for some couples, that's all there is to their quick engagement; no spousal obsession or sex-driven decision making, it was simply that they found someone to marry, and logistically it just made sense, which is a perfectly good reason. God awakens the desire for marriage in us, and there's no biblical command that says we have to take our sweet time making that decision and putting a ring on it. Some relationships need to simmer a little bit in a deep fryer, and some need to be put in a microwave before they are ready for marriage. That's okay. I know some couples that seemed like they jumped the gun, making an extremely eager decision, which has turned out to be fantastic. They didn't need to wait that long.

Both short and long-term dating relationships require hard work to make them work. Time is not an indicator of how much work needs to be done before engagement; work will need to be done regardless. If God awakens a desire within you to get married, then by all means, go after it. "He who finds a wife finds a good thing."[10] But we must be aware that whether we get into marriage at hare or tortoise speed, we need to be faithful within it. Marriage is a picture of God and His Church, and just as God isn't leaving His bride for anything, neither should we seek to separate from the spouse we enter into a covenant relationship with.

Those who have gotten into Ring by Spring engagements commonly voice their frustrations with the labeling and judgment received from friends, family, classmates, and even strangers. Regardless of whether you, as the outsider, think their decision was wise or not, you should not be shaming or looking down on these young, engaged couples. Close friends, mentors, and family members are the ones who, if anyone, should be addressing the couple if there is a legitimate cause for concern, but we should not look at couples who get engaged quickly with judgmental glares. If our reaction to their rushed engagement is concern, perhaps we should pray rather than prowl in judgment. After all, we want marriages, regardless of their dating length, to be ones marked by faithfulness and growth on account of both parties involved, right? Instead of condemning couples, pray for wisdom in their engagement and marriage.

Is there an ideal time to be dating before engagement or marriage? Each situation is different. There is no one size fits all answer for whether people should take the ring by spring philosophy or if people should wait longer, not wanting to rush into serious lifelong commitments. The amount of time it takes for two people to get engaged is for them to determine. While I may be shocked by the suddenness of their conclusion, I typically applaud when people get engaged out of excitement to see two people venturing out together.

Philippians 2:4 carries some profound wisdom for us all: "Let each of you look not only to his own interests but also to the interests of others." Quite simply, celebrate others and the things they have going for them. A good way for us to grow in contentment is to shift our focus from a when will my time come mentality to a that's amazing for them mentality. When we become more concerned with the well-being of others, we often find ourselves more content, less envious, and less comparative. A decision may not seem very wise, but our sincerest hopes should be that we are proven happily wrong rather than hoping we will eventually be able to say, "I told you so."

While it is ultimately up for the two lovebirds to decide, I can offer the advice that each of us should be patient and cautious, taking the time to assess our motivations and consider the future and the person we are going to spend that future with. Are we making hasty decisions because we are caught up in the culture around us where people are getting married left and right, or are we making these decisions out of love and a desire to be committed in a covenant to someone for life? Do we understand the mission? Whether a sprint or a drawn-out marathon, run well, run faithfully, and run lovingly.

In Response To The Romance

The answer to the romance around us is not to shame people for getting into relationships or for getting engaged young. We can have kind conversations with people about motivations but to condemn someone for moving along speedily in a relationship shows jealousy and immaturity on the part of the one judging. To caution people beforehand about eagerness is very different. A practice my mother taught me is that if it is late at night and I see a deer getting ready to cross the road, I flash my lights at oncoming cars to caution them about the dangers ahead. Having conversations about over-eagerness to get married is not that different. If two people want to get married fast or slow, that is their business. Like I said before, some select individuals should be the ones to speak into the relationship if there is something of concern to speak into. Judging people for getting married quickly simply because you disapprove of it is not a reason to condemn and shame someone.

Even if every young single person in the world read this book and assessed their motivations, ring by spring would still occur, couples would get engaged quickly, and there would be people who go their entire academic careers and maybe their whole lives single. So how do we deal with the pressures that make us feel like failures if we do not meet the deadline of finding a spouse by graduation or before we hit thirty? How do we manage the expectancy to find a person to spend our life with before we get a diploma in our hands? The answer is not to ignore the problem but to fixate on God, focus on the eternal rather than the temporary, seek to honor Christ no matter the circumstance, and remind yourself often about where your true worth comes from – not from the hand that is holding yours but from the hand that created yours.

Discussion Questions

In what ways, if any, have you felt pressured by Christian Dating Culture?

Is community important? Why or why not?

How do you think community should look? What does a Gospel-centered community look like based on the example of the early church?

Are you invested in community? If not, what is keeping you from investing in community?

What is your typical view of Ring By Spring?

Do you think that a person's worth is often associated with their relationship status? Why or why not?

Chapter 3: Over Spiritualization

In terms of dating, the two most dangerous times of the year are Valentine's Day and New Year's Eve. These holidays are heavily romanticized in our society. If we do not have someone to take out on Valentine's Day or a person to kiss as the ball drops on New Year's Eve, then it seems like we are missing out on a euphoric experience that appears universal. All of the couples you see on social media do not help with the feelings of exclusion and loneliness. The drive to experience what we fear we are missing out on often leads us to make unwise and eager decisions. I am no exception.

The night before Valentine's Day my sophomore year of college, I laid in my bed, staring at the ceiling. In my mind, I was going to be the strong, independent single who did not need anyone to make them feel whole. But in reality, I knew that I wanted someone to take out and show affection for on Valentine's Day. I'm a hopeless romantic, what can I say? I ended up flipping a coin several times, relying on what I perceived to be a sign from the universe to determine whether I would try to shoot my shot with my campus crush I had commonly thought about. When I got six tails in a row, it seemed like a clear sign from God that it was meant to be. The night ended with what I assume was a panic attack, a bit of heartbreak, flowers going to waste, and a stomachache from coping by consuming the bag of candy I had gotten for her.

My point in telling that story is to highlight my part in the practice of over-spiritualizing and looking for a grander meaning behind every detail to attempt to tell my fortune. The coin flips could have happened the other way just as easily. I was searching for meaning and direction from inanimate objects instead of looking to scripture for what to look for and prayerfully basing my decision on that. Relying on "what the universe is trying to tell me" focuses on circumstantial commonalities that are highly subjective, unreliable, and formulized. In our dating and relationship-obsessed culture, we tend to bend things in an attempt to see something that isn't there or force them to become something they aren't. We will reference the rare exceptions to try to make them seem like the norm.

One observation of mine is that we as a culture can easily prematurely identify something as a prophetic vision or word when it is often just a general statement fueled by our preferences. We can misunderstand our fantasies, dreams, or desires as being a sign from God. For example, someone daydreaming or sensing that God is telling them their future spouse will be tall is probably not a prophetic vision but rather an exposing of their preference. We have too often said that God is saying something or pointing us to something because that is what we want, trying to make our desires be marked as God's declarations.

Thinking Before You Speak

Have you ever randomly been confronted about something you've been saying wrong for a long time but had no idea you were saying it wrong? Whether it's adding an extra letter, mispronouncing a word, or getting an expression wrong altogether, you would be surprised at how frequently we misuse phrases without a second thought. We don't notice it because everyone is saying it wrong, so we can't know what's right. For example, many people say "I could care less" when what they should be saying is "I couldn't care less" because the former denotes that you at least care a tad while the latter implies that you don't care at all, which is the intended point of the expression. Many aren't aware of their incorrect usage of the phrase, which signifies that they don't know what they are saying in the first place.

Similarly, Christian dating culture contains several popular phrases and mindsets that we use that don't make sense. Distorted, unbiblical, or just plain foolish phrases are normal to hear. We assume that since everyone is saying it or sharing it on social media, it must be true, which is not always the case. These expressions I am referring to muddy the waters of dating cultures, hurt people, and sometimes go so far as to blaspheme.

This section will be about looking at a few of these over-spiritualized phrases and concepts that raise an eyebrow because of their potential ability to lead people astray in healthily approaching dating. All of these expressions I have listed will deal with breaking up, but they are often used in other ways. If you have used some of these expressions in the past, it does not necessarily mean you had malicious intent, but I want to make you aware of the implications of the expressions we use and how they impact the people on the receiving end. These are not numbered in order of severity.

1. "God Told Me..."

Just about everyone I know has had their finger pricked at the doctor's office for bloodwork. It's a universally recognized hurt that many have gone through. The Christian dating culture equivalent of something hurtful that many have been on the receiving end of is "God told me we should break up" or "I feel like God is leading us in different directions." These cards people play almost instantly cause confusion and frustration. One of the biggest disservices you can do regarding dating is blaming God for things not working out.

The usage of the "God told me" phrase has created a hesitancy to trust within Christian dating culture. Putting words in God's mouth has fostered spiritual manipulation into some wings of the culture and has added a layer of confusion that should not be there. This isn't just some pet peeve; the over-spiritualized, manipulative, and inauthentic use of this phrase is an actual hindrance to the health of Christian dating culture.

When you use the dreaded "God told me..." excuse, you run the risk of harming another person's faith as they begin to wonder why God articulated something so clearly to you but completely left them out of the message. Chances are, you could tell your friends the exact reasons why you wanted to end things. But instead of adequately communicating those reasons like a mature person, you used your apparent superior connection to God that you somehow possess as a scapegoat to avoid awkward conversations and confrontation.

Over spiritualization as a means to avoid conflict is an immature disservice that exhibits bad theology. Placing the blame on God to avoid responsibility and confrontational conversations is a practice I call "scapegoding," and it is venomous because it provides little to no clarity. It's scapegoating but shifting the blame onto God. Instead, communicate your major reasons for not wanting to continue a relationship. The clarity may hurt, but its sting lasts significantly shorter than an over-spiritualized, confusing cop-out. In regards to breaking tough news, some ways are better than others, which is why word choice and tone should be carefully thought through. Perhaps not every reason ever needs to be listed, but rather just the major points; use discernment on what to include and how to include it.

The proclamation that God whispered into your ear that you should end things with somebody is a bold claim and puts the person you are breaking up with in an awkward position. Even if God verbally instructs you to break up with someone, it is still best to confess your reasons outside of God and be honest instead of misleading. A trusted mentor once told me about a previous relationship where he was considering proposing but swears that he heard an actual voice tell him to break up with her. He had no reasons outside of that voice to break up with her but could not shake that voice, and so he did even though it seemed foolish. Come to find out, the girl had been cheating on him. Just because I have never heard an actual voice does not mean it never happens, but what I liked about my mentor was that he took responsibility for the breakup instead of just shifting the blame onto a voice he heard. While he would have been truthful in saying that he heard a voice, it was still better for him to take ownership. Taking personal responsibility instead of blaming God shows maturity.

Realistically, there is a good chance you are interpreting your emotions and your uneasiness as being God talking to you. We become so confident in our emotions that we sometimes elevate the message we think our gut is telling us to a level reserved for God's word, and that's not okay. God's Word is fully trustworthy and unwavering. Your feelings and emotions are the exact opposite. Feelings are important and helpful, but they are not always reliable.

In scripture, God spoke personally with people like He did with Moses and Abraham, and He also spoke through prophets such as Malachi and Isaiah. God also spoke in unclear ways to guide people, as He did in Acts 13:2: "While they were worshiping the Lord and fasting, the Holy Spirit said, 'Set apart for me Barnabas and Saul for the work to which I have called them.'" I describe this as "unclear" because it is unclear to us. Scripture doesn't say how He said all that, it just says that He said it. Scripture does not spell out for us what this looked like.

I've never had God say something directly to me. When people say "God told me," I always want to ask them what kind of accent God has just because I've never heard an articulated voice to be able to know. I don't want to "limit God" by saying it's not possible but walking in obedience to the wisdom of what God has already said in scripture is more reliable than a supposed special revelation.

The church in Acts adhered to scripture and walked in obedience. Follow that example. Hold your conclusions loosely and check them against scripture. When we hold our conclusions with the utmost confidence that God is the one explicitly communicating them, we run the risk of putting words in God's mouth. In Deuteronomy 18:20-22, Moses lays out the Lord's policy on false prophets: "But the prophet who presumes to speak a word in my name that I have not commanded him to speak, or who speaks in the name of other gods, that same prophet shall die.' And if you say in your heart, 'How may we know the word that the Lord has not spoken?'— when a prophet speaks in the name of the Lord, if the word does not come to pass or come true, that is a word that the Lord has not spoken; the prophet has spoken it presumptuously. You need not be afraid of him." In the same way that you don't want someone saying that you said something when you didn't, God commands us not to say He said something if He didn't. The consequence for doing so was severe, as you will see if you read the Old Testament.

If you believe God is trying to communicate to you through your feelings, perhaps change your phrasing when saying so. For example, Dr. Bobby Conway recommends substituting "God told me" with phrases like "I'm wondering if God is leading me in this direction."[1] But in the example of breaking up with someone, it is probably best to be honest about your lack of interest in the person rather than giving them a bunch of fluff reasoning or blaming God.

2. "I just don't have peace about this"

A friend of mine went on a date with a woman that he had liked for a while. Things seemed to have gone great on their first date, only for him to tell me a week later that she did not have peace from God about the relationship, so things ended. In his mind, that was a good enough reason to end things, and since he couldn't be upset with God about it, he moved on without it affecting him all that much. Months later, I heard the girl discussing with her friends about him, not in a gossiping way, but in an honest way, talking about some stuff from their date. She articulated to her friends that she found him to be weird, which is ultimately why she ended things, although she did not articulate that to him. Her explanation that she "just didn't have peace about the relationship" was a vague cover-up for the fact that she had actual reasons for not wanting to continue things. But instead of providing that clarity, she provided an over-spiritualized response.

Much like "God told me," saying I just don't have peace from God about this is often a "scapegod" term used to spare someone's feelings and shift the blame onto their apparent deeper communicating connection with God to avoid uncomfortable conversations and confrontations. Suppose you truly are uneasy about a relationship. Why don't you just say that to the other person and vocalize your disinterest rather than concluding that if God wanted you to stay, He would steady your heartbeat and regulate your breathing?

There very well could have been an uneasiness in a person's stomach about the relationship. But who is to say uneasiness is the basis for something being wrong? Roller coasters are a prime example. At King's Dominion in Virginia, there is a Dale Earnhardt-themed ride called Intimidator 305, which could not be more appropriately named. You can hear the screams. You hear the stories of people blacking out as they go down the massive hill. To say the least, you're intimidated. After riding it for the first time, my brother Alden had a paralyzing stare and just kept saying "305-foot drop" repeatedly as we walked back to the car. The nerves we felt beforehand were natural. Nerves are not necessarily a sign from God that something should not happen.

A bride and groom are nervous on their wedding day, but that doesn't mean the groom should leave the bride hanging at the altar. If that feeling of uneasiness is prolonged for an extended period or if you just can't shake that there may be something off, then there may be some legitimacy to that claim, but you should look to the root of why there is excessive uneasiness. I'm not entirely discrediting the telling nature of uneasiness, as I have ended relationships in the past because of that uneasiness I could not shake, but usually, there is something to point to for the cause of that uneasiness.

Pastor and author JD Greear sees "...nothing in Scripture telling us to look for peace in our hearts as proof the Spirit is behind something... But what about the 'peace that passes all understanding' Paul refers to (Phil. 4:6-7 NKJV)? If you read the context of those verses, you'll see that 'peace' comes from reflecting on God's fatherly promises to provide for us, not as a warm fuzzy from the Spirit when he's happy about a particular choice. This peace is the result of a trust, not a litmus test for confirming which choice is right."[2]

If you don't like someone romantically, just tell them that. If there just isn't a click between the two of you, even if it is just one-sided, then you should articulate that to them, preferably in person. It may sting to be told that someone does not like you back for whatever reason or maybe even for a reason you actually can't articulate, but that's a lot better than blaming the subjective butterflies in your stomach and your lack of sleep on God. If it's a genuine fault in their character, by telling them what it is, you give them something to work on. My friend had no way of knowing that some of his practices were off-putting because the girl had given him no clarity on what he needed to alter. Look to help others' futures as well as your own by communicating honestly, but use discernment for phrasing and tone.

3. I've Prayed About It

Bible-abiding believers would be wise to raise an eyebrow of concern at the sight of this section's title. We are constantly encouraged from the pulpit, from mentors, songs, and scripture itself to pray, which I am in total agreement with. Prayer, much like sleep, is constantly the thing we always attest to feeling the vibrant need for but can never seem to get enough of. But even a great practice like praying can become problematic if we start to use the fact that we prayed as God's stamp of approval on how we feel post-prayer. A great deal of manipulation can come from brandishing the fact that you prayed about something to get your way. We pray over a decision and then have the nerve to put the authority of God on the conclusion we come to.

In his book *Just Do Something,* Kevin DeYoung warns that "...we need to be careful that we don't absolutize our decisions just because we pray about them. Church boards and denominational committees are often guilty of putting their decision out of reach because 'the matter was bathed in prayer.' Certainly, prayer makes a huge difference. I am more apt to listen to others or be listened to if there has been a season of earnest prayer. But impressions of the Lord's leading after prayer are still impressions. We cannot infallibly judge the rightness or wrongness of our plans based on the feelings we have about them after prayer."[3]

When dating, you'll likely encounter someone who insists on praying about whether to continue going out with someone. At first glance, this seems like a sign of spiritual maturity, which it surely can be. But what happens when they had a great time yet went back to their room, prayed about things, and overthought every detail only to conclude that since they don't have peace, then God must be answering their prayers by not having something miraculous happen to say contrary to their feelings? We can overthink ourselves out of good things.

This is not to say that we should not pray about relationships. Part of the careful consideration of a person is bringing this person before the Lord in prayer and asking for His will to be done in their life and yours, all while begging for wisdom and eyes to notice things that are amiss. What I am not for is confusing our overthinking for being God's articulation and weaponizing prayer to turn down someone.

Aside from seeking wise counsel who will give you honest advice without a hidden agenda and looking to scripture to see if they meet even the basic scriptural requirements, ask yourself post-date, "did I even like being with them?" and without too much overthinking, base your decision to go on a follow-up on that. Don't use the lack of a regulated heart rhythm and uneasiness after praying as your basis of decision, promoting your feelings to God's word. Furthermore, don't use the fact that you prayed about something as a weapon to whack somebody over the head. Renew your mind in God's truth, seek wise counsel as you go along, but make your own decisions.

4. We Can't Date Because I Want To Work On My Relationship With The Lord

My disdain for this phrase is rooted primarily in four separate factors: the frequency for someone to seemingly change their stance soon after, mistrust in the sincerity of the phrase due to overuse and inaction, a fundamental misunderstanding of where growth can occur, and a delusional expectancy to fully arrive at readiness at some point.

Few things cut right to the core more than when someone tells you that they wanted to work on their relationship with the Lord and then to see them going out with someone very soon after. By very soon, I'm not talking three months or a year, I'm talking about the very next week. If all it takes for you to grow in your relationship with the Lord is a week, I am almost positive that most reasonable people are willing to wait that long. Look, just be honest with someone if you are not interested in them. Don't try to dodge the awkwardness of actually saying you're not interested in someone by cloaking it in Christian lingo. They are not entitled to a date, but the decent human thing to do would be not to pretend like you have a righteous reason and instead just tell them the real reason. "Honesty is the best policy."

Second, while it may be a legitimate reason for some, I have found through conversations and observations that many people will say that they want to work on their relationship with God but will do nothing to promote growth. There's no additional time devoted to prayer or reading scripture, no fasting, or anything of the sort. They misled you by telling you that they valued another relationship, but with their actions, they communicated that they only value it on paper and not in practicality. This dishonesty turns a legitimate reason into an insincere way to spare feelings. If anything, telling someone that you want to work on your relationship with the Lord only to not actually work on that relationship shows that you do need work. Too bad no work is actually being done.

Third, the notion that the only place where a person can grow is in singleness or isolation is silly because it is not as if growth becomes stagnant once a person starts dating or gets married. Singleness is not the sole arena where someone can grow in their walk with God. Those in a relationship, married or otherwise, can grow as well. Part of the reason the Bible carries such a strong emphasis on community is that being around godly influences molds and transforms you. If someone were to say to a congregation, "sorry guys, I can't go to church anymore because I'm trying to grow closer in my walk with Christ," we would all give them puzzled looks because God wants you to grow both individually and in community. We are not meant to be islands, and growth does not only occur in isolation.

Paul doesn't shy away from acknowledging that married people have divided interests.[4] Those who are not built on a firm foundation may find themselves neglecting their God-interest because they are concerned for their spousal interest. Individuals in relationships are tasked with more responsibility to which they must attend, all the while prioritizing God and honoring Him with those responsibilities. They may not be as free from the anxieties of worldly things as a single person is, but that does not mean that they cannot still grow in or glorify God while in their relationship.

Lastly, my opposition to this phrase comes from people's assumption that by working on one's foundation with the Lord in their singleness that they will be completely ready for relationships. On the one hand, it is extremely wise to build a strong foundation on the Lord before dating, and I would advise doing so. God is to be the priority no matter what stage of life you are in; both your singleness and relationships should be propelled towards glorifying Him.

But on the other hand, you need to realize that it's not like the microwave beeper will go off and suddenly you are fully prepared for everything a relationship is going to throw at you. You will never reach the full, perfect capacity of what you need to be as a part of a relationship. No one has ever reached that elusive peak. Married people aren't even fully ready for marriage. How would I know as someone who isn't married? Talk to any married person, and they'll tell you that marriage is hard work and there's conflict involved. You don't need to be married to know this. While no one is ever fully ready for marriage, relationships themselves have the potential to grow you closer to being what you should be, even though you will never fully arrive. As I elaborated on earlier, growth is not limited to singleness. Some lessons are only learned from experience.

In the last few years, I have grown in my appreciation for mixed martial arts. These fighters are some of the most disciplined, athletic, and poised wrecking machines in the world. Through years of training and studying, mixed martial artists learn how and where to kick, the proper application of submissions, how to grapple, and all the complexities of fighting, but there are some things that they cannot discover or learn how to do correctly without getting in the octagon or on the grappling mat themselves. Through diligent studying and learning from those who have trained before them, they build up a good foundation for what they need to do before they ever put on the gloves, but there is an opportunity to learn and grow inside the octagon just like there is outside of it. And even with all the experience and preparation in the world, they are still going to mess up and are still going to take a hit.

My guidance for you is to build a solid foundation before getting into relationships. God is to be the priority, which stands as truth regardless of where you go or what you are doing. But realize that relationships offer the possibility for growth just like singleness does, and you will never get to a place of being fully ready for a relationship, even with all of the foundation building in the world. I would hate to see you continuously not pursue a godly woman or not say yes to a godly man because you feel like you need to reach someplace that you can never actually reach.

Use discernment and be honest about where you are in your walk before considering whether to get into a relationship or pursue one. Also, be very careful about who you are trying to pursue or who you say yes to because a person can either spur you on in your relationship with God, leave you stagnant, or slow you down.

A Caveat

There are situations in which all of these phrases can be legitimate. God may actually articulate to you that someone is not a person you should be with. Your complete lack of peace is overwhelming and seems to only get worse the more that things progress. You prayed about it and found that they do not match up with scriptural imperatives. Maybe you want to work on your relationship with God because you feel like you do not have a good foundation or feel as though this other person may be more of a burden to your growth rather than an aid to it.

My encouragement would be not to use these or any other cliché phrases but rather sit the other person down and clarify how you feel and why you feel that way. Technically, no one is entitled to an explanation. Still, the kind thing to do is to clear up any confusion.[5] I want to clarify that it is understandable to use these phrases to distance and protect yourself in hectic situations that may involve concerns for your safety. Still, generally, you should seek to be sincere in your reasoning and try not to blame God for what could be based on your feelings. Usually, lying to a person hurts more than the truth in the long run, but remember to be diplomatic, gentle, discerning in your truthfulness, and above all, honor God.

One Last Phrase Worth Addressing

Initially, I had planned on only covering the previously mentioned phrases. But as I closed up my writing for this book, I remembered a phrase not used for breaking up but rather for getting together and when exactly that will happen. Although it takes many variations, the sentiment "whenever you become content in God alone, then God will send you a spouse" grinds my gears because it sets up the false notion that somehow we can manipulate God into giving us what we want through our contentment.

As Paige Benton Brown puts it, "'As soon as you're satisfied with God alone, He will bring someone special into your life—as though God's blessings are ever earned by our contentment."[6] I imagine that this phrase came after seeing some people develop a sense of "if it happens, then it happens" towards dating and then soon after found themselves in a relationship, but those exceptions should not be reduced down to a guarantee.

First off, God is not moved to action just because I chilled out. He is not mine to command or manipulate. He is not a genie. Second, I can easily see how this mentality could lull us into feigning contentment, essentially lying to ourselves, to gain what we believe is promised on the other side. Third, the confusing logic of "don't desire something to get it" pits us against desire, as if having the desire for something is wrong. So long as something is not desired more than Christ or goes against what God has laid out in His Word, having a desire is perfectly fine, and we shouldn't have to pretend like we don't want it to try to get it.

Aiming at being content so that God will give you a spouse comes across as very "name it and claim it" prosperity gospel-like. As if sowing the seed of contentment would produce our desired outcome because God somehow exists to do our bidding. Preachers and singles conference speakers will proclaim this phrase from the pulpit, and while they may be calling people to a good thing like contentment, they are calling people to be content for the wrong reasons. Contentment in the Lord should be present because we love the Lord, not just because we want what He could potentially give us.

Honestly, this phrase often comes across as prideful because it insinuates that someone arrived at some magical point in which they were content and considered worthy of a spouse by God, similar to what we talked about in chapter two. The sentiment is often vocalized by people already in relationships, so the connotation is that they got to that mountaintop. Part of my issue with this is that I know several people of remarkable character and faith who exhibit no active interest in relationships but wouldn't mind being in one, and yet in all the contentment they display, they still have never been "sent" a spouse. This is because God does not owe us anything because of our contentment.

I have seen people who are just as anxious as ever get into relationships, and I have seen people who are fine with where they are at in their singleness find themselves in a relationship. Proverbs 18:22 encourages us that "[he] who finds a wife finds a good thing" with the keyword in there being finds. Whether we can find contentment for the day as we trust in the Lord[7] or wrestle with the anxiousness of life, scripture seems to beckon us to seek contentment out if we want it. Some will encounter a relationship that seemingly falls into their lap; others will have to be intentional in initiating the relationship. God often works in the weirdest of ways and the oddest of timings. But while many content people do find themselves encountering a relationship that they were not expecting, their contentment did not contractually obligate God to hand them a significant other.

This over-spiritualized phrase, as well as the others we have talked about, needs to be cycled out of our vernacular and replaced with biblically-based, loving, honest, clarity-giving language. The culture has developed sentiments that either set false expectations or give misguided reasons, and as a result, we are often left frustrated, confused, and sometimes even spiritually downcast. Christians, knowing the most incredible love there ever was, is, or will be, should be able to tap into that to be able to give loving, truthful reasons for wanting to break up if there is a desire to, and should sincerely look to not manipulate spirituality as an easy escape out of a relationship. As hard as it may be, the loving thing to do is to be clear and honest, as uncomfortable as that can be. But whoever said that loving people would always be easy?

Discussion Questions

How would you describe God's voice and direction?

Do you feel like your standards are too high or too low?

Does any form of nerves instantly mean that God is against the decision? Why or why not?

In what ways, if any, do you think prayer gets used as a manipulation tool?

Chapter 4: Want a Word? Read the Word

In the last chapter, I wrote about how over-spiritualization impacts Christian dating culture. We want to hear from God, which is not a wrong desire, but where the dating culture gets complicated is when people ignore written scriptural wisdom because they are trying to decipher what they perceive to be God's voice. Part of the problem of Christian dating culture is that people don't know what to look for or ignore that which tells them what to value.

Instead of looking for a sign, clinging to our feelings, or trying to notice coincidences to tell us who to date or marry, we should look to the general wisdom found in the Bible. No, it won't blatantly say "you should propose to Kiera" or give you an exact list of things a spouse has to have, but there is guidance to be gleaned. Certain things are valued over other things throughout scripture. And so, with that knowledge that comes from scripture, we can filter through the things that are not specifically listed but surely must be considered.

After all, "The fear of the Lord is the beginning of wisdom, and the knowledge of the Holy One is insight."[1] Through biblically saturated decision-making and wisdom filtered through scripture's lens, we can make better choices. Christian dating culture needs a decision-making skills overhaul that begins by reforming around what the Word of God says about what to value. Basing our decisions on the truth of scripture instead of coincidences and butterflies in our stomach is one of the cultural pivots we need to foster a healthier dating culture.

Here are some things to consider. First off, do you even like being around this person? Are you friends, or can you at least see yourselves becoming friends? Would you want to be their friend even if you did not think they were attractive? Would you recommend this person as a friend to someone else? If the answer to those questions is yes, that's a good sign. These aren't directly biblical questions, but these are just some good beginning questions to consider.

Do you find them attractive? Yes? Wonderful. Next, assuming you are a Christian yourself, are they a pursuing Christian? Also, yes? Off to a magnificent start. I'm not trying to be contradictory by asking about friendship and attraction before the question about faith. Both of those things you should probably be able to tell pretty early on, which is why I asked those questions first. I'm not sure who said it first, but I agree with the sentiment that attraction should be on your list, but not the core of your list.

Do they love God and their neighbors?[2] They're not going to get it perfect, and neither will you, but is there at least a pursuit of that? Excellent, they sound lovely. Do they seek to exemplify faithfulness, love, hospitality, kindness, and a good work ethic?[3] Does their present character and the pattern of their life indicate that they will actively pursue obedience in their respective role as indicated by Ephesians 5:33, which says, "...let each one of you love his wife as himself, and let the wife see that she respects her husband?" You have to be a critical thinker here and have high but realistic standards.

Have you looked into their recent history, discovering patterns about their behavior and relationships? Have you sought wise counsel[4] from trusted friends or mentors, communicating to your significant other your concerns over red flags that have come up and asked for their side of the story? How do they treat the people that don't necessarily have anything to offer them?

Still wondering what to look for? Read the story of Ruth and Boaz. Although Ruth is not a book of the Bible solely about marriage or singleness, I still believe some wisdom can be gleaned from its pages concerning those matters. Note that not a single word of the four chapters in Ruth indicates a radiating attractiveness from either party. Does that mean they weren't attractive? Not necessarily; Ruth evidently had an appeal to her because she was married before she met Boaz. The Bible isn't fixated on their physical beauty. The book of Ruth highlights Boaz and Ruth's mutual appreciation for each other's outstanding character. Ruth exemplified loyalty and showed a compassionate heart for the brokenhearted.[5] Boaz was hard-working, generous, and kind.[6] He obeyed Deuteronomy 24:19, where God lays out the miscellaneous law to leave the forgotten sheaf in the field for the sojourner, fatherless, and the widow. Boaz looked out for Ruth's safety.[7]

While to me it's apparent that there was an attraction present – you'll find that guys typically are going the extra mile for a girl they think is cute – Boaz and Ruth's character is what stands out the most.

They weren't perfect, but there was a reverent adherence to scripture and a love for others. Overall, we can gather from their story that character is monumentally important, it matters how someone treats strangers, making your intentions clear is not a bad thing, and that motivated pursuit is something we should model.

From examining their character, we see that each of them could see the growth that could come as a result of being with the other one. Their evaluation was practical. They would be good for each other, helping each other to thrive. Boaz showed incredible kindness, and Ruth showed outstanding commitment —if each absorbed the traits of the other, then both of them are better off as a result of each other's company. These two, who certainly hit it off as friends thanks to initiatives of kindness, had character that would help the other grow in their affections for God. They pointed each other to the character of the Creator through the way they treated one another.

Ultimately, marriage is a picture of Christ and the Church. As John Piper remarks, "The divine reality hidden in the metaphor of marriage is that God ordained a permanent union between His Son and the church. Human marriage is the earthly image of this divine plan."[8] Is the person you are considering getting into a relationship with the type of person you can trust to honor that divine reality and edify you in the Word? If the aim of dating is finding someone to be our spouse, then the cultural motivation should be centered around the key questions, and I believe that question is the most important one to consider.

It's just a first date

Now that we have addressed some of the things to look for, it's time for some nuanced conversations about some topics that are bound to come up as we go on dates or consider going on dates with someone.

In my observations, I have seen many in Christian dating culture decline a date or not pursue a date because they are concerned that the person they are going on a date with might not match up to scripture, but they are determining that before even going on the date. How can we determine if someone does or does not match up with scriptural standards unless we give them a legitimate shot? This is why I am such a big advocate for not putting pressure on first dates. When the expectation from both parties is that nothing is demanded or expected and a first date is simply a time where both people can get to know one another without any sort of expected commitment, it frees both parties up to relax and enjoy. There should be intentionality behind a date but not an expectancy. Keep the wisdom that scripture offers at the forefront of your mind as far as what to look for, then go on a date and just see where it goes. If it goes nowhere, that's fine! Your worth isn't decided by whether or not it works out between you two. If it goes the distance? Celebrate! But still know that they don't define your worth.

I can see where someone could get pretty frustrated with going out on a date with someone only to find out that it was not going to work out, leaving both parties feeling like they have wasted their time. This is why my most prominent suggestion is to get to know someone before asking them out. Whether it be in group settings, being friends beforehand, or simply having a conversation with someone before asking them out, an excellent way to avoid being surprised is to be familiar with them beforehand. Being familiar or going in not knowing much are both fine places to be, but ideally, you would know what they are like before going out. It's just a first date, not a marriage commitment. So relax and have fun as you get to know someone.

Checklist

Backpedaling a tad, I want to re-emphasize that we should have a checklist in one sense because there are things that we should be looking for in a person. But in another sense, we shouldn't be so ironclad with our checklist that no one ever has a chance. The necessity for discernment and standards does not invite judgmental legalism. You're imperfect, and the other person is imperfect as well. Yes, you want to look out for things that mark a person's character. No, you don't want to evaluate everything under a microscope and demand perfection because you're not going to get it. As Kathy Keller says, "...most people, when they are looking for a spouse, are looking for a finished statue when they should be looking for a wonderful block of marble."[9]

In chapter one, I alluded to Heather Thompson Day's father saying that decisions should be based on who someone is now, assuming nothing will change. Keller's statement and Thompson Day's father's statement do not contradict, by my understanding. You want potential in motion. No one ever fully arrives, but it's pretty obvious when someone is in a better place from a growth standpoint than someone else. Much like a recently drafted professional athlete, they should already be competent, but they could grow to be so much more.

It is not all up to the other person to meet your standards. Meet theirs as well. Don't put yourself above them; put yourself in their shoes and strive to be what you would want them to have if you were them. A relationship is not meant to solely please you because it is not all about you. You'll never treat another person the way you should if you approach the relationship thinking that you are the center of the universe.

A Word on Physical Attraction

As pointed out earlier in the chapter when I brought up Ruth and Boaz, the heart, faith, and character of a person matter when it comes to what to look for in a spouse, not so much looks. Were you to go blind tomorrow, never to see your significant other again, would you still enjoy their company and trust them to be faithful to you? Those are the types of questions that are much more pertinent than asking how their social media feed looks, how lucrative their bank account is, or how chiseled their jawline is.

Even though character is more important, a negative extreme that some spheres of Christian dating culture go to is proposing that all physical attraction considerations are petty and poorly prioritized. And while I can see some legitimacy to those claims in some situations, completely writing off physical attraction does not appear feasible and may be demonizing something that shouldn't be. Realistically, attraction is a factor. I don't think anyone is dying to not be attracted to their spouse. How many people do you know that just flat out have never been attracted to their husband or wife? But at what point does your lack of attraction to a person become a deal-breaker? The person you may not find physically attractive could be the godliest in the world, but if you shutter at the thought of kissing them, then I think there's a potential issue.

1 Samuel 16 is often referenced in the discussion on the consideration of physical attraction. As God said to Samuel, "Do not look on his appearance or on the height of his stature, because I have rejected him. For the Lord sees not as man sees: man looks on the outward appearance, but the Lord looks on the heart" (verse 7). This verse is often used to convey that looks should not be a consideration for those wondering what to evaluate in a significant other. I would agree that physical attraction is not the most important thing, but I would disagree with the total disregard of physical attraction in the equation.

1 Samuel 16:7 is specifically about picking the next leader for Israel, not a spouse. Physical appearance is not a paramount point of consideration for the leader of a kingdom. Leadership ability and character are. God saw the heart of David and knew that He was what Israel needed as a leader. But it's not like David was unattractive; 1 Samuel 16:12 describes David as being ruddy and handsome. The text went out of its way to say David had beautiful eyes. The leader of Israel during this time, King Saul, was notably handsome and taller than everyone else but lacked obedience and humility. It seems like the disregard of physical stature in 1 Samuel 16 has more to do with a contrast to how King Saul was than a total abandonment of considering attraction. The principle of how looks are not the paramount consideration can be gleaned from 1 Samuel 16:7, but the context does not specifically discuss spouses.

Song of Solomon takes note of character at various points, but chapter four clearly beholds the beauty of the beloved. Who would fault Solomon for delighting in the beauty of his bride? I doubt anyone would. Jacob worked a total of fourteen years for Rachel, who he found beautiful, but was not attracted to Leah, who he was tricked into marrying. Jacob was not in the wrong to appreciate beauty but would have been in the wrong had he been solely motivated by beauty, which is vain (Proverbs 31:30). Looks can be a consideration but they should not be the primary fixation.

Even the people who harp on how physical attraction should not be a factor likely passed up on somebody at some point. Chances are, someone throughout your life has been single and has displayed godly character towards you, and you didn't pursue them romantically. The first person to be godly towards you does not have to be your future spouse. It is reasonable and understandable for you to want to be attracted to your spouse, just don't value that over their faith and character, which I hope you will someday find to be attractive.

Keep in mind that attraction fluctuates as you get to know a person. I know of several couples that were friends before dating and were not attracted to each other in the slightest, but over time grew to find their significant other beautiful as they saw more of their heart. On the other hand, I know from personal experience that some physically attractive people have become less attractive in my eyes as I have gotten to know them personally. My policy is to give things an honest chance and just see where things go even if there is not a raging attraction element present because things can develop. But if attraction does not develop, then there is no harm so long as I communicated and did not try to play around with another person's heart. However, I could see an argument for not going on the first date to begin with if you knew you were not attracted to someone to not get their hopes up.

Prayer is necessary surrounding all things in a relationship. If you find yourself attracted to a person's character but not attracted to the face that holds that character, then take it before the Lord in prayer. Ask Him to reorient your heart to see God's craftsmanship behind this soul He knit together. If you find yourself still unable to get over the things that hold you back, don't stress as if they were your only chance at meeting someone godly. But take this opportunity to prayerfully evaluate your standards because if all you ever consider is a face or a body and then a heart further down the line, then something is off in what you value.

I'm not going to recommend just forcing yourself to look past your complete lack of attraction to someone just because you notice something godly. Who wants to be with someone that holds the opinion "you are not much to look at, but at least you're kind" about them in the back of their mind? I know I don't. Faith and character are monumentally more important than appearance, but we cannot be naïve and pretend that physical attraction is some blurry background actor who should be disregarded. Outward adorning, beauty, and charm have an expiration date while character and faith typically do not, so our decisions should be based around what has a longer shelf life, but a consideration of attraction does not make someone's standards entirely askew.

We're human. We're often trivial. I've heard something along the lines of this said: "You are the one that has to look at them the rest of your life, and if you can't get past something about them physically, then maybe you should let them go so they can find someone who doesn't mind or even adores the thing that seems to bother you." I'm not positive that this is the answer, but I do see the wisdom in knowing that there is likely someone out there who sees art where all you see is a few colors and some shapes.

To not see someone as attractive does not mean that they are not fearfully and wonderfully made. God created each of us fearfully and wonderfully in His image (Genesis 1:27, Exodus 4:11, Psalm 139:14). Scripture does not hide that humanity will not find all other humans attractive, but a lack of attraction should not mean that there is a lack of appreciation for God's intentional job of knitting us together. I do not have to find a creation to be beautiful to recognize that the artist did a good job making the art. My attraction or lack thereof towards someone does not change their inherent status of being fearfully and wonderfully made.

If you are going to get married to someone, you will hopefully be with them for the rest of your life. To desire that the person you marry is someone you are genuinely attracted to is not an inherently awful desire, but it should not take precedence over faith and character.

"You're just not good enough."

I feel as though I should address this head-on since someone is likely to abuse looking out for biblical qualities and turn it into a weapon against people. First and foremost, don't place yourself on a throne as the faultless princess or prince who has all of the kingdom having to come to your castle to prove themselves before they can court you. Get off your high horse. We all have things to work on.

Knowing that people are not perfect, we should be armed with grace, humility, and reasonableness, not with an axe of demanded perfection that we swing at those who don't meet our too-tall standards. I'm not proposing that you settle, but I am asking you not to demand perfection with a vice-like grip.

From the descriptions of what we should look for in a spouse, we see a standard we cannot live up to all the time. No person is loving around the clock. We are slothful, often more than we'd like to admit. We fall short of these standards because of our sin. But what God offers in response to our falling short is grace, and the same must be offered up from us when people fall short in being the type of man or woman we ideally would love to see pursue us. The grace we need to show doesn't ignore what is lacking, but it doesn't hinge everything upon the secondary issues.

The core essentials of active faith in Christ and faithfulness are the two non-negotiables, while just about everything else can be assessed and evaluated from there. Pastor and author Jonathan Pokluda remarks that "You're not looking for perfect; you're looking for practical. You're not looking for someone who's perfectly made for you because they don't exist, because you are so messed up. You're looking for someone who practically complements you so you can marry and serve God together."[10]

If I'm demanding perfection out of someone, if I'm demanding that they have to get everything right all the time, I'm going to be disappointed, and that person is going to feel an impossible weight to carry. Let the things that truly matter like their faith, character, and integrity, be your main points of reference, with secondary things being factored in but not being held to too high of a standard. If I'm breaking hearts or avoiding relationships or commitment altogether because I'm waiting for someone who has it all together, I'm waiting for a person who will never come (aside from Christ). Abandon your search for the perfect spouse because you'll never find them. Instead, embrace biblically-minded practicality and grace. Use that grace in the search for a person who pursues the things that truly matter: God and being a person of grace-filled character and integrity.

Singleness Isn't a Sorry State

While relationships are worth pursuing, I worry that a subconscious motivation for wanting to get out of singleness and into relationships is because we view singleness as a sort of lower state of existence, as if relationships are regal living while singleness is lowly.

Paul made it clear that marriage is not a necessity but is a gift: "Now as a concession, not a command, I say this. I wish that all were as I myself am. But each has his own gift from God, one of one kind and one of another."[11] Scripture backs up that marriage and relationships are not bad things to be in or pursue. Scattered throughout the Bible are commandments and wisdom concerning marriage.[12] Your life can be enriched by having a spouse, but it's not a need. Your ultimate need is Jesus Christ; He should be your number one pursuit because while marriage is beautiful, it expires at death or Christ's return. But Jesus is forever.[13] We should live for what has the most longevity and leverage the temporary for the eternal.

Being so obsessed and locked in on marriage distracts you from the purpose of singleness. Notice I did not say you must never marry, and that is the only way to be dedicated to Christ. What I am saying is that obsessing over your relationship status will distract you from serving and the rest of your life. Although it may not always feel like it, singleness is a time of flexibility and availability that enables you to serve and follow undistracted. Yes, the possibility of romantic love in the future is something we can look forward to and can rightfully be thrilled about, but it is not something that should rob us of living fully and presently in the moment. Romance isn't worthy of being God; God is. Fixate on Him, not your discontentment with your singleness. Your relationship status does not define your worth.

A Closing Thought

By following the wisdom that scripture provides on what to look for in a person, you may fool yourself into thinking that if you somehow find the perfect embodiment of the scriptural things to look for. Or if you find "the One" with whom you are totally compatible, it will remove all marital conflict. If you legitimately think that, let me ask you this: have you ever been around an actual married couple? The resounding pattern across all marriages is that it isn't easy. Songs rarely seem to depict it, but marriage and relationships, in general, are not a walk in the park. Conflict is rampant. You don't realize just how many things can turn into an argument. Throw kids into the mix, and you have another layer of complexity. Whether dating or marriage, it will not be smooth sailing all of the time.

However, the Word of God does not leave us hopeless. Although we can see it in little ways when dating someone, marriage overwhelmingly reveals selfishness and faults in both the husband and wife. In Psalm 139, the same chapter where David praises God for being fearfully and wonderfully made, David ends his writing with a plea to God: "Search me, O God, and know my heart! Try me and know my thoughts! And see if there be any grievous way in me,

and lead me in the way everlasting!"[14] Whenever I have prayed that end plea to God, He typically reveals my faults to me soon after in some way or another. And from that realization of my sinful ways comes the opportunity to turn and learn from them through the Spirit.

Outside of individual progression, a couple will grow from the conflicts they encounter together. As you learn together, heal together, fight together, you hopefully will come to know one another more and can care for one another better as a result. You learn where the other's pressure points are, and from there, you can figure out how to better love them in that area. The Bible is fully aware that we will get into conflict and therefore guides us through it:

- "Therefore, having put away falsehood, let each one of you speak the truth with his neighbor, for we are members one of another. Be angry and do not sin; do not let the sun go down on your anger, and give no opportunity to the devil... Let all bitterness and wrath and anger and clamor and slander be put away from you, along with all malice. Be kind to one another, tenderhearted, forgiving one another, as God in Christ forgave you." (Ephesians 4:25-27, 31-32)

- "Husbands, love your wives, as Christ loved the church and gave himself up for her... let each one of you love his wife as himself, and let the wife see that she respects her husband." (Ephesians 5:25, 33)

God knows we will get into conflicts with one another because we are insecure, want things our way, and most obviously, because of the impact of sin. Sweeping everything under the rug and pretending everything is as good as it can be is not healthy. When there is conflict, you will need to deal with it. You are not going to avoid conflict by supposedly finding the most compatible person for yourself. One of the best things to look for is a person who deals with conflict in a healthy way, not someone who just loves stirring up conflict or avoids it. If someone is realistic about the fact that there is a conflict within a marriage and trains themselves well to deal with conflict lovingly and healthily, that helps tremendously. Conflict is inevitable, and you will want someone who will stand by you in the storms, lock arms with you, and faithfully brave the winds to push through to the other side.

The Bible has never been shy about the realities of human conflict. From family conflicts found in Cain and Abel to evident relationship issues in the church in Ephesus, it's clear to see that issues are inevitable due to living in a fallen world. But by looking at the struggles of others, we can learn healthier alternatives and glean the characteristics that would have aided the biblical characters in their time. We can only learn scriptural wisdom if we read it. Far before we hinge everything upon the subjectivity of feelings, we should cling to the Word of God and wring out what God has to say about our situations. If you're seeking a word from God on how to navigate the situation you find yourself in, romantic or otherwise, open the Word.

Discussion Questions

What do you typically look for in a person?

How important is physical attraction to you when assessing someone romantically?

Is what you typically search for in a person lined up with what the Bible values in people?

For those in dating relationships: If you were not dating the person you are with, would you want to be friends with them/recommend them to one of your friends?

How does the culture around you make you feel about singleness?

What are some non-negotiables you have for a relationship?

Chapter 5: The Aesthetic Influence

Social media needs no introduction in the twenty-first century. To meet a person who does not currently have any social media accounts feels as rare as a Bigfoot sighting, and meeting a person who has never been on social media is even rarer than that. Admittedly, there has been a lot of good that has come out of social media, such as revolutionizing marketing, allowing individuals to connect and keep up with loved ones, and introducing new ways to let vast amounts of people learn valuable information. But for every pro of social media, there is a con; mental health decline, discontentment, addiction to virtual stimulation, a struggle to be present in the moment, among other things.

On a recent trip to the magnificent Grand Canyon for the first time, I was blown away by the depth of the natural visual masterpiece. After taking a few minutes to enjoy the view and even shedding a tear or two, it seemed like the only natural thing to do was take a few pictures to capture the moment. But the pictures were not solely for my enjoyment and reference. I knew that ultimately I was taking them to post them on social media later to convince others that I am living a remarkable life.

Not every social post is to portray to the world how great my life is, and I want to be careful not to make all social media posts out to be doing so. Some posts are to show appreciation for a time, person, or organization, and other times it is to make myself laugh or let others contribute to a memory. But too often, I find myself posting to be seen and shape the outside perception of myself. My reasoning for taking photos at the Grand Canyon serves as a larger representative commentary for culture at large: what we do and why we do it has drastically changed due to the influence of social media. I am not intending to shame people for using social media, more so aiming to start a conversation about its impact.

The biggest mess maker in terms of dating and relationships for our modern-day has to be social media. Like I alluded to in Chapter 3, the two worst days of the year to be single are unanimously Valentine's Day and New Year's Eve because of how romanticized those days are in our minds. That's not to say romance is the enemy or that people should not be romantic on those holidays, but the celebration of those holidays and the overwhelming amount of posts on those days does have a cultural side effect. Scrolling through social media on those days makes it seem like everyone is on a date, everyone got a kiss as the ball dropped, and we rang in the New Year, and everyone got proposed to. At times, this has infested my life by making it hard for me to be happy for other people. So the question then becomes, am I just going to allow these things to keep hurting me, or am I going to do something about it?

On the other side of the rainbow for the potentially infectious nature of social media is our tendency to fool ourselves. Too often, a person will continuously post about how great their relationship is or how great their significant other is, but once they break up, behind the scenes abuse comes to the surface. The smiling pictures we post to try to broadcast to the outside world that everything is okay is sometimes an attempt to convince ourselves that everything with the relationship is excellent while deep down we know the person we are pictured with is emotionally manipulative, holding us back, or maybe is even downright abusive. We don't have to show the world a beautiful casket to distract them from the fact that there is something dead inside.

Do I think that social media is entirely pointless and a terrible thing? No, but what I don't want is for a good thing to turn bad. I don't want to be plagued by longing and live for likes from crowds of people I probably do not even know that well. Perhaps if we were not so invested in our social media presence and deceived by the person we portray online, dating would reach a level of ease it hasn't experienced in years.

Social Media and Christian Culture

Christian culture tends to deviate from the secular societal norms of what you may see on a social media profile. While all people who post tend to do the commemorative photos at a sports game or concert or a collage for someone's birthday, I have noticed that Christians tend to highlight relationships more than the secular world. Sure, the secular world appreciates a nice engagement photo as well, but the Christian aesthetic seems to be one that really wants you to know that they are dating, engaged, or married. Of course, this is not true for all Christian circles or all Christians. But in the social spheres I have studied, I have observed this to be common. Christians and anybody else should rightfully be excited about dating, engagements, and marriages, as these are beautiful things to celebrate. Often the posting is just an overflow of genuine love that people can't help but share, and I am not faulting people for that. But I bring this conversation to the table out of concern for our obsession with relationships and the cultural impact that obsession has when it gets carried over to social media.

The frequency of relationship posts and building of aesthetics around a significant other commonly found within Christian circles speaks to the cultural obsession with marriage that I have written about throughout this book. Suppose we tie our worth to our relationship status. In that case, logically, we will broadcast our relationship developments to let the world know we are loved and desired by another human being. Unfortunately, it often seems like we cannot count ourselves truly happy unless we can aesthetically prove it.

The conversation that needs to take place is one that asks what we are hoping to accomplish with our social media presence. If no one else knew about our relationship developments, trips, and triumphs, would we feel like something is missing because we did not post about it? Perhaps Christians need to shift from the societal norm of finding our highest affirmation in likes on social media to the biblical foundation of finding our worth in the love of our Creator and Savior. I am not outright condemning posting about relationships on social media. I am simply trying to raise this concern and start a conversation about it, expecting each to draw their own conclusion and wrestle with their own informed convictions. Consider your motivations, discern the outcomes, and proceed in wisdom.

With social media, we are broadcasting something to the world. No matter what we do, we are always sending a message. Will that message seek validation and love from the world, or will our message come from already knowing that God loves us? Social media is a powerful tool to reach people with the Gospel and to inform others about causes we care about and events we'd love to share, but let's be cautious about finding our worth in it and be mindful of the impact that comes from it.

Photography Sessions

I want to preface this section by saying that there is nothing wrong with taking pictures with others. Photos capture a moment forever to be used as a valuable memento. Being someone with numerous friends who are wedding, elopement, or engagement photographers, I do not want this section to come across as a cease and desist for their business ventures. This section is simply an analysis of the effect that the services their customers purchase have on the dating culture at large and a beckoning for us to consider if this particular activity is beneficial.

Engagement photo shoots are seemingly a necessity for our generation. The posed portraits give a glimpse into the wedding that is to come; the transition from ordinary apparel worn during an engagement to the wedding attire is a beautiful parallel. Although engagement photo sessions are not essential, they are nice to have, and it is nice to see engaged couples getting excited about their conjoined future. And we as spectators should celebrate that which is worthy of celebrating.

What raises an eyebrow from a cultural analysis standpoint is when couples who are not engaged get engagement-level photoshoots together early on in their relationship. The pictures may be nice, but I believe that some unintended consequences of the practice include making breakups (if they are to happen) harder due to the intimate nature of photoshoots, an expectation of engagement is often set up in the minds of the models, and an inevitable contribution to the "Ring By Spring" mindset is made.

One of the most challenging elements of a breakup is the galleries of pictures together on a camera roll. Having photos with a person that things are now different with is like being haunted by a ghost. Throughout high school, I had several friendships fall apart, and then pictures I had from back when I was close with someone plagued my happiness because I had a still frame of when things were as I wanted them to be. But I knew that the present reality was significantly different than how things were in the picture. Of course, risk is always present with attachment; it's just part of the human experience. But I think there is a vast difference between capturing a photograph that commemorates what has been built versus capturing a photograph of something that has not happened yet and may not happen.

While ordinary pictures taken on a phone camera or polaroid can undoubtedly pester us with their memories, an intimate, professional photo seems that much harder to get over. As the picture quality increases, it captures the innermost idiosyncrasies of a couple, seemingly deepening the bond of the precious moment. Were a breakup to occur, having special photos with a significant other can make it that much harder heartache because there is a visual representation of what could have been had things progressed to the point of engagement. This is not to say we should not ever take pictures together or that quality photo sessions are inherently bad, but we should be aware of the potential for how much harder a breakup can be as a result of having a glimpse into what could have been. There's a vast difference between a photo taken on a smartphone to capture a moment at a concert and a professional photograph where you are intimately wrapped up in someone's arms.

When taking an engagement-level photoshoot with a significant other, the dynamic of the relationship turns from "I can see myself getting engaged to this person" to "I have a visual picture of what it would be like to be engaged to this person," which I believe sets up a potentially unhealthy expectation of engagement. It's like we are given a glance into the future, and then knowing what we suppose is in our future, we set our expectations that things will get to that point, which we are not guaranteed that it will. Suddenly, the relationship carries the assumption that things will go from picture to reality. 2D to 3D. The expectation we have built up in our minds could hurt even more if the foundation is pulled from beneath us.

As relationships progress in time, there logically comes an assumption that things will one day get to a point where the next steps are taken, and commitments are proposed. But developing that expectation very early on in a relationship bears the burden of expectation that may blind us to red flags because we fixate on the seemingly promised status of engagement.

During my last semester of undergrad, I got the opportunity to take a survey of songwriting literature class. My tendency to jot down lyrics made the class a logical choice. One day in class, the professor remarked how many young artists have gotten scammed by record labels because in their fixation on the status of being a signed artist and the wads of cash waved in front of their faces, they eagerly signed to a contract that benefited the record label far more than it helped the talent.

The artists were given an image that showed them their desires and hastily signed a contract that they did not understand nearly as well as they needed to because they were promised a status with some flashing lights. Such is what can potentially happen to a person who is given a stilled frame that shows them practically engaged but without the ring, which the photo sets up as an expectation.

A key distinction to note is that this is guidance against professional photoshoots really early on in a relationship, not a prohibition of all professional photoshoots while dating. It's inviting people to consider holding off until there's some ocean behind you. Everyone feels on top of the world when spirits are high as a new ship embarks off from the harbor, but the voyage truly worth celebrating is the one that celebrates even after the adrenaline has worn off, some tides have been navigated through, and the crew still loves each other even though they've been out at sea for a while. That's why it's called a relationship (pardon the pun.)

By professionally photographing relationships in the beginning weeks of a relationship, I believe this directly leads to an influx of ring by spring engagements. Subconsciously, when everyone around you seems to be in a relationship, a tendency to want to be in a relationship and be at the same point as everyone else develops, which may lead to progressing through a relationship quickly. As discussed in a previous chapter, getting engaged quickly is not inherently a bad thing because there is no exact timeline for when a couple should get engaged. But some alarms are triggered by rushed engagements due to the tendency to overlook the seriousness of the covenant and negative traits of the other person because of the state of adrenaline that lovebirds typically are in at the beginning of a new relationship.

One Last Thought

This is not a prohibition of any photo session together before engagement or marriage. This is a plea to have a conversation about motivations and expectations that come from intimate photo sessions with a significant other. Maybe for the sake of wanting to save yourself some potential heartache and spare your mind some relational expectations, you and your boyfriend or girlfriend should wait on having an intimate photography session together until more than a few weeks have passed.

Is there an exact moment where it becomes culturally okay to take a professional photo shoot together? No, just like how there is no spelled out moment at which a person should get engaged. Ultimately, no one has jurisdiction over what the exact timing should be. But that's why this is a necessary conversation to have with friends or significant others. The day may be today, or it may be months down the road, or it may become discovered that it is not necessary for your relationship at all. The important thing is that you consider what expectations you are setting your relationship up for.

Discussion Questions

Do you think that Christian dating culture has a "picture perfect" obsession?

Are you a fan of taking "engagement-level" photoshoots before getting engaged?

How has social media impacted dating and relationships in general?

While engagement-level photoshoots at the very early stages of a relationship are permissible, are they beneficial?

Chapter 6: The Motivation Rarely Admitted
Purity

Before we dive into the topic of the motivation rarely admitted (it's sex, in case you were wondering), I want to address purity because I feel there is a great deal of confusion surrounding the topic. Purity is a taboo word for many in the modern world, and while I think there are plenty who abuse it, make it out to be something it is not meant to be, and whack people over the head with it, I don't believe the concept is something inherently awful.

Sex Ed is one of the most awkward and jaw-dropping courses you'll sit through in your life. During the Sex Ed portion of my high school health class, my fellow students and I watched a video on the miraculous nature of birth and my health teacher, a comedian, after having us watch the VHS tape of the birth - which was already way more graphic than what I thought labor was like – decided to rewind the tape, so we got the joy of watching the baby go back in. There's a sight you won't unsee. Sex Ed communicated to me the seriousness of sex and its potential byproducts. Pregnancies happen, even in high school. STIs were and are a real thing. Our hormones are ricocheting off the walls like a pinball game as we develop, which can drive us to make eager decisions. All of this and more made me conclude that it was best to wait until marriage to have sex, which aligned with what I was taught from the Bible growing up.

It wasn't until high school that I even had my first kiss. But once that first kiss happened, I just wanted more. I had been waiting for this my whole life, with everyone around me always getting in relationships and me just sitting on the sideline, only being able to dream of what it was like. But now it was here, right within my grasp, and that was all I wanted. Soon it was just a lot of making out with my then-girlfriend, with it being communicated that we were not going to go any farther than that, and it never did. But I was just fine with doing what I wanted, knowing full well I was being lustful but defended my actions in the name of "well, at least I'm not having sex." Coupling a relationship that is mostly about making out and a teenager who was wrestling with a pornography addiction in the fourth grade is a recipe for disaster. I wasn't even looking up pornography. I was just replaying images in my head and acting out fantasies my lust-fueled imagination had taken me to. But hey, at least I wasn't having sex, right?

At the time, I wasn't even a Christian. But when I understood grace for the first time and could even remotely wrap my head around what Jesus did on the cross, I still was wrestling with my lustful habits and all the shame that came with it. That first relationship ended, and eventually, two other girls came into the picture about a year apart from one another. Both were kind to me but were not Christians at the time, and there were things about them that I just overlooked because I was attracted to them, and they were attracted to me, which was something I was not used to. The affirmation I craved when I was younger in the form of someone finding me attractive fueled my embrace of lust because it was a childhood dream come true, a desire finally fulfilled. I was all over the first one, and she was all over me in the back seat of her car, "but at least I hadn't gone too far," was the way I rationalized it in my head. Grinding with a girl at a Halloween party led to a date a week later and us making out in my truck, but "we weren't having sex, so it was all good" was what I told myself to justify my actions that I knew were leading me deeper into lust and deeper into my pornography addiction. I was making every provision for the flesh I could. They were not to blame for my pornography addiction, but what I was doing with them was not helping me at all.

There came a point where I had to sit back and realize that giving ammunition to my lust was only hurting me. In my mind, I was fine because I hadn't gone all the way and gotten burned by the fire. The hair on my hands was charred off, but at least I was still a virgin, right? Thankfully, I eventually realized that it was not all about seeing how close to the fire I could get before I got burned. It was about respecting that fire, others, myself, and the purposes for which each of us was created. The fire was not destructive in and of itself, and intimacy is not the enemy, but the way I distorted what the fire was made for resulted in years of hurt. My desire for intimacy and to be seen as wanted moved me to participate in things that linger in my mind and alter my view of God's creation. The affirmation I was craving was found in what God says about me, but I was too concerned with what His creation was trying to tell me.

Fixated on the status of virginity, I forgot all about the purity God had called me and others to. Author Mo Isom, whose story and my own share some similarities, puts it like this: "God cares deeply about the obedience and purity of the hearts that carry [His] light. He cares about the heart of each person long before He cares about their actions. Because our actions are what grow out of a pure or impure heart. When our hearts are pure, our actions become pure. And when our hearts are impure, our actions follow suit... What happens as a result of understanding why we are called to purity? Virginity and abstinence become the by-products of a heart that seeks to honor God. It's about so much more than doing what's right and avoiding what's wrong... A pure heart compels us to make decisions that don't seek first to please ourselves but rather to please a holy God."[1]

Obedience is important, but the motivation behind it is also important. If it's obedience for the sake of "don't do wrong," it can be legalistic, but if it's obedience out of love for God, in pursuit of purity, and wanting to guard our hearts for the sake of pleasing God and reflecting His truth, trusting His intentions, design, and authority, then it's heartfelt devotion. True purity is rooted in Romans 12:1 "I appeal to you therefore, brothers, by the mercies of God, to present your bodies as a living sacrifice, holy and acceptable to God, which is your spiritual worship." It's a desire to be set apart for the sake of loving and knowing God as well as making Him known. We will fail in this effort to always present ourselves as living sacrifices, but thankfully God has afforded grace to us.

Where I think purity has failed people is the insinuation that no one will want you if you have had sex before marriage or that somehow you are spoiled goods for having had any intimacy or sexual experiences, consensual or not. Let me emphasize this: you are not less valuable in the eyes of God if you have had sex before marriage, and you are not more valuable if you have not had sex before marriage. I was not dirty or undesirable for having made out with those girls back in high school, and neither were they for making out with me. Those who have been burn victims from the misuse of the fire are still beautiful. We were and are still afforded grace. We are still loved, and that didn't change at the sight of sex. Were you to regain your virginity somehow, you would not be more saved if you had never lost it in the first place. Morality and sexual purity do not determine your place in

Heaven. We need to reorient the conversation about purity into one that stands on scriptural truths about seeking to be faithful but also preaches the forgiveness and restoration found in Christ alone for all our sins, sexual or otherwise.

The Design of Sex

If there's one thing that the non-Christian world and the Christian world can agree on, for the most part, it is that sex is good. Barring any traumatizing experiences which sadly do happen, sex is generally seen as one of the better things people get to participate in. I can say that even as someone who has not had sex simply because science shows us the chemicals that go off in our brain during sex and the intentional placement of nerve endings on specific parts of the body points to the pleasurable nature of sex when properly used.

God made sex. It was not a science experience gone wrong or a blooper in His design. Sex is something that God has gloriously gifted humanity not only for procreation and bonding but for enjoyment as well.

The Bible puts a yield sign up before we can dive into enjoying this enjoyable gift. According to the pattern of scripture, God's design is for sex to be enjoyed between a husband and wife within the borders of marriage. 1 Corinthians 7, which addresses the fact that married couples should have sex to fight off the urges of sexual immorality, uses language that directs that sex is for a husband and wife. Not a boyfriend and girlfriend, not two friends who are just into each other, not an engaged couple. A husband and wife. Genesis 2:24 says, "Therefore a man shall leave his father and his mother and hold fast to his wife, and they shall become one flesh." – Jesus echoes this in Mark 10. Sex is a deeply intimate, beautifully designed, spousal unifying delight meant for husband and wife to enjoy together.

What's the Motivation Behind Your Matrimony?

The summer before my senior year of high school, I had never heard a sermon on sex. Sex had only been mentioned in sermons about sexual immorality, so I never really got to see the positive side of sex. I was astonished when my youth pastor Jim preached on the Song of

Solomon (aka Song of Songs). I would always skip over the Song of Solomon, thinking that it was a hymn placed in the middle of the Bible. As Jim would show me, Song of Solomon is a poetic back and forth between two people who are madly in love with one another.

After that night, I started to notice the frequency of talks, podcast episodes, sermons, books, and more centered around the topic of sex. Out of all the ones I listened to or read, they spoke very highly of sex. An unintended side effect of the rise in talking about the pleasure of sex is that people will, I believe, set their sights and motivations a little too much on it and expedite whatever is needed to get it sooner, whether knowingly or unknowingly.

For a person wanting to obey scripture, it would appear that sex is Point C, with the unmarried being at Point A, and the only way to get to Point C "the right way" is through Point B, marriage. Those with their sights narrowed in on C are going to want to leave A fast, get to B, so they can finally reach C almost immediately after. The overemphasis on Point C has resulted in some people getting to Point B way before they grasped the purpose of Point B.

Paul knows the draw towards sexual immorality is strong, even saying, "To the unmarried and the widows I say that it is good for them to remain single, as I am. But if they cannot exercise self-control, they should marry. For it is better to marry than to burn with passion."[2] But I don't believe that what Paul is suggesting is getting married because your primary motivation behind marriage is sex. To want to rush into the covenant of marriage just because you want to have sex views the other person as a means to an end rather than as a beloved person. A person's humanity is likely lost in the haze if all you view them as is the path to sexual satisfaction for yourself. If the first sign of sexual desire were the indication that we need to get married right that second, then frankly, I should have gotten married at the ripe age of thirteen. The presence of any sexual desire does not mean that you must get married to the person it is directed towards, nor is it a green light that you have to get married as soon as possible.

As author Christopher Yuan points out, "Too many have taken Paul's words out of context: 'It is better to marry than to burn with passion' (1 Corinthians 7:9). The Corinthians were spurning marriage while engaging in extramarital sex, and Paul chastised their lack of self-control and motivated them to consider marriage as a good option. When speaking to high school and college kids, I often tell the young ladies that if their boyfriend wants to marry as soon as possible because he doesn't want to 'burn with passion,' they should run as fast as possible away from a man so lacking in self-control. The same is true for boyfriends being pressured by their girlfriends to quickly marry so that they can have sex. Wanting to have sex is not the right reason to get married."[3]

Fuel to the Fire

Looking at this "burn with passion" discussion from a different angle, I want to highlight a distinction. There probably is a natural sexual desire present within a relationship due to our human nature, and that is primarily what I am speaking to when I say that the desire for sex is a factor in the decision to pursue marriage but should not be the primary motivator (more on that in a few paragraphs).

But over time, I have heard it vocalized that the desire for sex has become too powerful to the point that it forces someone's hand into pursuing marriage sooner. There could be a variety of reasons for this enhanced burning desire, and I won't attempt to dive into all of them, but I will address one factor that we mostly have control over.

While the "fire of desire" is present, what are we doing to pour fuel on that fire to make it too hot to handle? What I mean is that I hear people complain about it being so hard to pursue purity with their boyfriend or girlfriend, and yet they actively watch pornography or make out in the back of cars. No wonder it's so hard to try to fight the good fight; you're putting yourself in harm's way. It's like sitting near a sprinkler and complaining that you got wet. I do not want this to get confused with some "purity culture" prohibition of all physical contact or intimacy, as if somehow you are broken, impure, or damaged if you have kissed someone or held a hand. But what I am saying is that we should be mindful about what we are doing that is making it harder on ourselves to wage war against lust.

All I am saying is we should think through our convictions, assess what tends to cause us to stumble, and pluck it out, much like

Matthew 5:27-30 teaches. Like I discussed earlier in this chapter, I used to give in to making out with different people because it filled a void. But after wrestling with that conviction, knowing where it took my mind and how it impacted the war on my lust, I came to the conviction that making out is something that I should not do before marriage, and I would advise others not to out of reflection on my own experience. But I can understand if someone else does not hold that conviction, in the same way, that while some hold convictions about kissing before marriage, I do not (there are vast differences between kissing and making out). While I can't hold all people to the same convictions I have and judge them, I can look to see what scripture has made clear and have grace-filled conversations about these kinds of convictions.

I am not instantly condemning things such as premarital kissing. But if an individual holds a conviction about it, then it is wise and beneficial to steer clear of it. Again, intimacy is not the enemy, and I am not attempting to demean or shame anyone who does what I have convictions about. But I am trying to lovingly start this needed conversation that pleads with people to think through their actions and determine what could be wiser, more beneficial alternatives. Our aim is not to give ammunition to temptation. We aim to serve our brothers and sisters in their war against lust by not being a stumbling block for them or ourselves.

A Factor but Not the Determining Factor

Sex is not the entirety of marriage anyway. David Marvin of The Porch says this: "In a given year, if you have sex four times a week for 30 minutes each time, you will spend 1 percent of that year having sex in marriage. That means 99 percent of the time you're spending with that person; you're not [having] sex."[4] Why are we so motivated and entranced by that 1%? (I sound like Senator Bernie Sanders.) The desire to have sex is a factor in the decision to marry someone, and not all sexual desire is lust, but sex should not be our primary fixation.

If you're just looking to be with someone sexually but not willing to serve them, comfort them, listen to them, grow with them, pray for and with them, and lay down your life for them, then you're not looking for marriage. You're just selfishly looking for someone to satisfy your sexual desires. If you as an individual are just looking to get married for the sake of having sex, then you are not viewing the person you would want to marry as a person, and more importantly, as a creation of the Most High, you are viewing them as a sex object and not as a spouse. The entirety of another person's existence and partnership with you in marriage is not to sexually satisfy you.

If the sexual element was delayed or not nearly as present as you might think it will be, would you still want to get into marriage at the pace you are planning? Sex is surely something to look forward to, but it's not as much of marriage as the culture would commonly make you think. Therefore, it is best not to be motivated by a good act that is a minority part of the whole.

Talking About The Taboo

My largest desire with this book is to start conversations about Christian dating culture. Thankfully, people were contacting me to have crucial conversations even before this book came out. On one particular occasion, a friend of mine called to discuss a plethora of topics, one being her recent discovery that her newlywed friends were not having nearly as much fun on their honeymoon and in the first few months of marriage as they thought they would. For some of those newlyweds, it was an issue of dealing with the transition of being taught all your life that sex was evil but then getting married and it suddenly becomes your best friend. For others, the issue was not their view of sex, it was the actual act that was the issue.

In our cultural emphasis on sex, the nightmare of sex potentially being an unpleasant experience has barely crossed our minds. When sex is made out by the culture to always be this euphoric escapade, the humanity and reality of the act often get pushed to the side. The fact of the matter is that sex can be a painful or unsatisfactory experience for some, which no one seems to talk about. Although I am not married, these eye-witness reviews speak to the common theme I have heard over the years: sex isn't always the fairytale that it's often cracked up to be.

Aside from dealing with the emotional or psychological pain that can come with sex (which I do not feel qualified to try to tackle in this book), the physical discomfort some experience is a rarely discussed topic. Sexual organs are sensitive and elaborate parts of our bodies, and the changes that come towards them when we begin to have intercourse can result in some pain as things alter and adjust. Fear and trauma can even play a part in making the experience painful, uncomfortable, or even retraumatizing. If you just think through the act logistically and with even some basic medical knowledge, you should be able to figure out how sex may be painful at first for some people.

This speaks to two necessary responses: patient understanding from the spouse and a realistic view of sex that includes knowing that while God's design for sex is beautiful, the adjustments to getting to a point where it is pleasurable can be difficult. By thinking of sex as always being great for both parties all of the time, we are neglecting to recognize the complex humanity behind the act and risk causing pain, being insensitive, or even inducing pain unintentionally upon our spouses. The important thing is that the two of you listen to each other and your respective bodies, seek to benefit the other party, communicate, and lovingly display patience with one another as you navigate the complex and yet beautiful gift of sex together.

The honeymoon is a much-anticipated getaway for a newly married couple. But the conversation that never seems to happen is the one that talks about how people often aren't batting 1.000 their first time. From simply listening to the stories of newlyweds and thinking through things logically, it's easy to see that the first few times may not be the greatest experiences. I am not trying to be grotesque by discussing a taboo topic like sex and sexual performance, but I feel as though it is a needed conversation since it seems like many have unrealistic sexpectations. Just because you waited to have sex until you were married does not mean that you'll be good at it.

This whole section was uncomfortable to write partially because we are not used to having these much-needed conversations. Not that every relationship talk should turn into a sexual discussion, but people simply are not having any conversations about sex, so they go into marriage unprepared for the complexities ahead. By lacking nuanced dialogue about the discussions people are most eager to have, the culture is not setting people up to thrive. We need to steer away from the delusion that sex is always pleasurable, accessible, and uncomplicated and have the necessary talks about the taboo topic to set people up for success. Sex is beautiful, but making it an idol that we neglect to recognize has complexities is a gross disservice to Christian dating culture.

It's okay to recognize that sex isn't always as advertised. But even if it isn't all that you were told, are you still going to be faithful? Are you still going to actively care for them even if the experience isn't what you thought? If the pain of adjusting to sex results in sex being withheld for a time while they navigate through healing, will your pursuit of them stop? Alongside our commitment to the covenant we set out on with our spouse, we should be committed to holding a realistic and understanding view of sex and treating the taboo topic with great care and sensitivity.

The Divorce Phenomenon

Throughout writing and advertising this book on social media, I was blessed with the opportunity to talk to countless individuals about their experience with Christian dating culture. What shocked me most was the number of people I encountered who had gotten divorced relatively shortly after getting married. In my conversations, numerous individuals confirmed or theorized that their hyper focus on the good gift of sex prompted them to jump into a commitment with someone that they did not know or desire, but they saw as being a means to the end of sex.

I struggled to write this part of the book because I feel like many people wrestle with the desire to expedite the process to experience sex in what the Church typically teaches is the approved setting, but they won't admit it. From my introspection, I can attest to the struggle of wanting to take my time in a relationship but also know that if I rush through things, then I can finally experience what has for so long been emphasized as the prime marriage benefit. In the language of 1 Corinthians 10:13, I assume that this struggle is common to man, and I am not an isolated incident. I sincerely doubt I'd get honest survey answers if I polled people on whether their horniness was the main motivator for their hurried matrimony. But with all the emphasis on waiting until marriage for sex, there have to be people out there that rush into things just so they can have sex. I worry that in the fast-forwarded approach motivated by sexual desire, we may overlook red flags we are blind to.

The only way I can figure to address this issue is to ask these questions: was sex your primary motivation, even if deep down, for getting engaged and eventually married quickly? Are you taking your time to evaluate the character of the person you are seeing, or are you tossing that to the side because you are trying to get yourself to a place where you can finally have sex? Do you like being around them, or do you just like the idea of being with them sexually? Do you understand the covenant you are getting yourself into?

This isn't an insinuation that every couple that gets engaged or married quickly is motivated primarily by the desire for sex. This isn't an attempt to discredit the fact that the desire for deeper intimacy with another person is a legitimate factor in the decision to marry someone. Nor is this an invitation for people to get divorced if sex was their primary motivator. This is merely a conversation starter, a billboard on the side of the road that poses a question and asks that you genuinely consider it as you continue to drive. Maybe you can honestly say that the want for sex is not your primary motivator, so you can keep on trucking down the road. Maybe this billboard makes you slow down and alerts you to just how fast you're going. Or maybe, this caution alerts you so much that you have to pull over to the side of the road, take a breather, and contemplate your motives for your destination and speed of travel. Nothing is in and of itself wrong with getting to your destination fast or slow, but there could be something off about the reason why you want to get to your destination at the speed you are going.

I don't want you to get from this chapter that sex is something we should give a disapproving side glare to. Sex was God's idea, so the furthest thing I want to do is speak against something God designed. But what I do want to make clear is that while sex is a part of marriage and it is a good thing, it is not the main thing. Marriage is a great thing, but it and its benefits are not ultimate, and we should not put sex and marriage on a pedestal in our lives because even these wondrous creations made by God fade in comparison to God Himself.[5]

Discussion Questions

Should sex ever be the basis of a relationship?

Has sex been overemphasized for Christian dating culture? If so, what do you believe is the reason for that?

How common do you think divorce amongst Christians is? Why do you think that is? (This is not intended to be judgmental or to look down on those who have, this is to ask the question and start a nuanced conversation about some of the reasons why.)

How has purity culture impacted Christian dating?

What are some personal convictions you have about boundaries for romantic relationships?

Are there any fears you have associated with sex? If you feel comfortable sharing, what are they?

Chapter 7: Flexing Faith

"'Beware of practicing your righteousness before other people in order to be seen by them, for then you will have no reward from your Father who is in heaven." (Matthew 6:1)

The necessity for a day of rest never made sense until I graduated college and found myself craving a nap endlessly. When sleep-deprived, I tend to reflect on the things I could have done differently to ensure that I would get the most sleep, and most of the time, my conclusion is that I needed to escape the YouTube rabbit hole I often find myself falling into before bed. The algorithm pushes a plethora of videos onto my screen, from theology debates to basketball highlights, but a video of someone helping a homeless person gets recommended now and then. While the act of helping someone down on their luck is wholesome, the savior complex that often comes across from the person helping the homeless is bothersome. Of course, we should appreciate charitable giving and hospitality as a society, but when character and actions are projected for selfish gain, the mission seems skewed.

As we discussed in an earlier chapter, there are certainly things to look for within a person. But a risk we run with making godly things (such as faithfulness, serving, worship, etc.) prominently "attractive" in Christian dating culture is people taking on those characteristics and broadcasting them to seem more attractive within the culture. Or, unfortunately, you will get people that fake their way through those characteristics to appear like they have it all together. Much like the content creator who posts about their generosity towards the poor, the caring act and character displayed are undermined by the performative philanthropy. The display of character and care has become more about the person giving than the cause or person receiving.

Within Christianity, I call this performative broadcasting of godly characteristics and biblical obedience "flexing faith." Unfortunately, flexing faith is hard to detect. The primary difficulty around identifying flexing faith is that we do not know people's hearts or motivations, so self-evaluation is key. Each of us must look at our hearts and identify our motivations for advertising our faithfulness and fruits, not necessarily an obligation only to inspect others. I am ongoing in deciphering why I do the things that I do, and I encourage you to do the same reflectively, currently, and proactively.

We put Bible verses, or CS Lewis quotes in our bios. We wear church merch, work at camps, go to conferences - we do so much that proudly states that we are Christians, which is a tremendous thing to be, and the Gospel is a paramount thing to share, but what we need to consider is the reason why. Why do we want to share so much about our faith? Is it because we want people to hear the Gospel and come to know that their sins are atoned for by the precious blood of Jesus, or are we broadcasting Christian parts of ourselves because being a Man or Woman of God (MOG or WOG) is the most attractive thing a person can be in Christian dating culture? Are we doing things to be seen by others, or are we doing them for the cause of Christ? Are we chasing Christ or chasing Christian clout?

Why do we pose with children we encounter during foreign missions trips for photos and post about how we thought we'd change their lives but really, they changed ours? Why do I have to share with all of the social media-using world that I woke up and did my devotion this morning? These can all be things that have no blatant ill-intent behind them, and some genuine encouragement can come from them, but the question still needs to be asked: are we using the good works we do in the name of Christ to try to build up names for ourselves?

There have been times that I have interrogated myself, questioning my motivations. I've driven myself nuts wondering why I raised my hands during worship when I know that's typically not something I do. Did I just do it because the spiritual people around me do it, and I have heard girls say things like, "it's so attractive to see a man passionately worship God"? Am I showing off my faith simply because I know what is perceived as attractive within the culture, or am I doing so because I want to be faithful and care more about what my Heavenly Father thinks? There is no way I am the only one who digs deep and tries to determine if my motivation is to make Christ known or to make sure others know that I know Christ.

Thank God that there is grace and a Savior who knew about my selfishness in advance and still went to the Cross.[1]

Worship Isn't Supposed to be Sexy. It's Supposed to be Worship

Throughout my time in the Church, I have encountered numerous people romanticizing worship leaders and the act of worship itself. First off, saying "it's so sexy when someone worships" is a tad weird to begin with because while worship leaders are individuals with dignity that should be seen, the objective of worship is to point to God, not to ourselves. For a worshiper to fixate on other worshipers rather than the One being worshiped misses the entire point.

Second, remarking that worship is an attractive activity can influence people to want worship to be seen rather than to be centered on the holiness of God. When we sexualize faithfulness, we risk influencing people to do all the Christian postable things such as working at camps, going to conferences, and posting their devotion to appear more attractive within the culture. Those things are perfectly fine to post when coming out of a love for God and a desire to see Him be known and not ourselves.

Good Motivations for Sharing the Good News

Much like the content creator doing good things for their public relations and income, people can do the right thing with the wrong motives. Spreading the Gospel is sadly no exception. In Philippians, Paul made it clear that he wants the Gospel proclaimed no matter what our motivations are because this good news is too important not to share. He even acknowledges that some proclaim Christ out of love, but some proclaim Christ out of selfish ambition.[2] It seems like some near Paul adopted a competitive mentality to proclaiming the Gospel, wanting to be seen as a greater leader or proclaimer of the good news than Paul (good luck). This selfish ambition that Paul writes about in Philippians 1 tells us that there was a problem with sincerity in faith and people flexing the Gospel for their gain even back then. We can be proclaiming the right truth with the wrong motivations.

Granted, Paul did garner some "Christian clout" through his church planting and evangelism. But, of course, you would have people talking about you too if you went through being beaten, shipwrecked, and imprisoned and yet still were preaching the Gospel to the very people who put you through it all. But that's the difference between Paul and us sometimes – he may have gotten a reputation, and people may have looked up to him as a result of his works for the Gospel, but his works were truly for the Gospel, not for man's empty praise. Paul's aim wasn't to pick up girls, for people to think more highly of him, or to build up a platform for himself, but rather it was all to point to Christ.

I want to make a quick note about the "celebrity Christian" conversation that has come up a lot more frequently in recent years as several popular pastors, authors, and teachers have been found to be involved in some sort of scandal. As much as I agree that we should have respect for leaders but not idolize them, where I differ from some is the notion that fame is the issue. Realistically, if you are extremely talented or knowledgeable in an area, you are likely going to become a notable figure, and so a great responsibility is placed upon those who possess a platform. If you become well-known because you are sharing the Gospel or preaching well, then that is fine. Several speakers throughout the Bible were well known in their respective times for their work for the Kingdom, but their motivation was not to be famous, but that was an outcome of their proclamations. So if by chance a platform is built as a side effect of your faithfulness, you are not instantly an egotistical jerk. But you are now entrusted with the responsibility of being in the public eye, which calls for accountability, humility, and integrity. Fame is maybe not something we should longingly seek after, but if it happens to come to us, then we simply must be faithful there just like we would anywhere else.

But what do we do if we realize that we are sharing God's Word and proclaiming Christ out of selfish ambition rather than love? We go back to the scriptures and root ourselves in the example of Christ's humility. We pray, we repent, but we don't stop proclaiming Christ with our words and lives. You are the only one aside from God who knows your motivation for putting Bible verses in your bio or getting cross tattoos. If you determine that your motivations were not rooted in love for the One who loved you first, then continue to share but take the time to ask God for a detoxification of your motivations and a reinvigorating of biblically sound motivations.

How Well Do You Know Them?

My persistent caution around getting engaged or married so quickly comes in part from my concern that people don't know the true nature of their significant other. The true self likely has not had a chance to become evident in the blissful, adrenaline-fueled beginnings of a relationship. Not that you have to know everything about a person before advancing in a relationship, but it makes logical sense to know what they are like, where their values lie, how you feel about them, and where you see things going after you have stopped walking on clouds and you've had a few not so easy days. While jumping into an engagement or marriage quickly can prove to be a good decision, there's also a chance that you aren't seeing the larger scope of a person at the beginning because they are keeping up appearances and still have their guard up.

I hear stories too often of couples who got married within a considerably short amount of time (without a history of friendship) and then got a divorce soon after. The list of reasons for why divorce happens can be long and range from adultery to "falling out of love" to realizing they did not even like the person because they were caught up in the puppy love of a new romance. Once people get past "I do," they tend to let their guard down, revealing more of their faults and maybe even removing the masks they had been wearing to try to impress their significant other. Relationships certainly do further reveal to us not only our faults but our significant other's as well. But I believe that for those who have been faking their way through faith to climb the ladder of social standing within Christianity, the realization that they are not like what they broadcasted is somehow even more detrimental.

An article by Lauren Vinopal for Fatherly revealed the risk rate for divorce based on which year of your marriage you are in. Years 1-2 and years 5-8 carry very high risk. "Today, the average length of a marriage that ends in divorce is eight years, according to several estimates, but that extra year may be due to the fact that the average divorce now takes one year to process and clear the legal system."[3] Although the article lists other reasons for divorce likelihood in those years, my hunch is that the reason for these spikes is because within those first few years, you go from the honeymoon phase to the adrenaline wearing off and the guards of both partners being lowered as they become more comfortable. Such a phenomenon reveals some of the true character that was not evident before. Vinopal also considers the factor of children, among other things, in the divorce statistics for years 5-8. Being a parent reveals a whole new realm of a person that was likely impossible to see before their children were born. The point is that as time passes, our true selves come to the surface.

These observations are not intended to somehow blame those who were not able to see the fakeness of someone else because they did not take a particular amount of time to evaluate. After all, some people are so good at faking things that it may take a significant amount of time to reveal themselves. But I bring these things up to bring awareness that people can be fake and often use the good name of Jesus to manipulate others, which spells trouble for the dating culture. Integrity should be a paramount pillar of Christian dating culture, something that we hold each other accountable to due to its crucial nature.

The conversations that need to happen surrounding flexing faith begin with an honest reflection about who we are trying to project ourselves to be. Are we honest with ourselves and others about what we are like? From asking ourselves hard questions like that and rooting ourselves in scripture, we can begin to see what we should be like and then cultivate real heart change through a growing relationship with Christ. We want to be people of biblical character, not just people who act like they have biblical character.

Let's say that you do happen to meet someone faking their way through life or faith to appear like they have it all together. While you cannot change a person's heart, you can encourage them to talk to someone. If it is a spiritual issue, then maybe a pastor. If it is a behavioral problem such as anger, then guide them to a therapist or counselor of some kind. You cannot fix them, you are not their Savior, but you can influence them to seek healing.

Space To Breathe

Have you ever tried to remain perfectly still like a statue? It is virtually impossible because our bodies aren't used to perfectly holding poses for extended periods. If we approach the assessment of someone in dating like looking at a wax figure so that the other person feels they can never show their shakiness in fear that they'll get caught and everything will get ruined, you're likely to see some people holding things together that are completely broken. Not only are you likely to see people hiding flaws and overcompensating to make up for them, but you are liable to eventually be caught off guard once you see their flaws poke their head out behind the closed doors of a marriage commitment.

In *The Meaning of Marriage,* Timothy Keller describes how those dating and living together have to keep appealing to their significant other to keep their interest. In comparison, Keller argues that a married person can let their spouse see their bloopers and not just their highlight reel because there is a "...space of security where [they] can open up and reveal [their] true selves. We can be vulnerable, no longer having to keep up facades. We don't have to keep selling ourselves."[4]

While I have elaborated on the importance of looking for genuine, unselfish pursuit of God, I don't want to accidentally communicate that people need to fake it until they make it to keep up appearances because they never feel good enough. You don't have to have it all together before getting into a relationship or advancing in one. We can't demand perfection. We can't make conditions so strict and grace so unfamiliar that people feel forced to fake things to pass inspection. We are works in progress who are being sanctified. There has to be room to breathe.

This doesn't mean that a person gets free reign to bask in their ungodly characteristics. But this does mean that if a person still struggles with something, there should be freedom after some trust is built to be vulnerable so that they don't feel the need to put a mask on. Just because they are vulnerable with you does not mean you have to like or approve of whatever they struggle or have struggled with, nor does it mean you should be their therapist. Also, their vulnerability with you does not contractually obligate you to stay in the relationship because it is a dating relationship, and you are free to end things. While some consequences may come from their vulnerability, there shouldn't be a toxic pressure on them from individuals within the culture to sweep all their struggles under the rug and only display the things we deem attractive.

As Keller comments later on in his book, "Within this Christian vision for marriage, here's what it means to fall in love. It is to look at another person and get a glimpse of the person God is creating, and to say, 'I see who God is making you, and it excites me! I want to be part of that. I want to partner with you and God in the journey you are taking to his throne."[5] Christ did a finished work on the Cross for us, but He is not done with us. We are being molded. Don't expect people to be completed buildings when they are still under construction. What you want to look for is someone under construction by God, whose foundation is secure on the Cornerstone, and who's being excavated of that which once took up residence and is being filled all the more with love for the Lord. There is work that still needs to be done but weighing the severity of those things that need work and mulling over their potential in motion, you might consider signing a lease.

What about their past?

"Love is patient and kind; love does not envy or boast; it is not arrogant or rude. It does not insist on its own way; it is not irritable or resentful; it does not rejoice at wrongdoing, but rejoices with the truth. Love bears all things, believes all things, hopes all things, endures all things." (1 Corinthians 13:4-7)

One aspect of God's grace that I appreciate thoroughly and constantly comfort myself in is the fact that God already knew about all of my sins before I even did them, which means that Jesus went to the Cross knowing I was going to hurt Him. The forgiveness and reconciliation afforded to me by Christ are that much sweeter knowing that God knows the entirety of me and yet still somehow wants me. God isn't holding my past sins against me because they are covered by the righteous, atoning work of Jesus.

But the reality of dating is that everyone has a past, some with more severe actions in them than others. In giving people space to breathe, we also need to create space to mindfully consider a person's past and how it will impact their present and future. In light of people's pasts, should that impact whether you pursue things with them in the present? What if they have a criminal record? There are some daunting things that people have done in their past that we should at least be mindful of because they are part of a person's story and could very well influence their present and future. There is no one-size-fits-all answer to this question because each situation is unique.

There's a pastor from my hometown who was once the largest drug dealer in the city. A lot of daunting things had happened throughout his life that had led him to that point, but it was still his choice to be a drug dealer. He had even served time in prison for fighting, which came after a history of violence throughout his life (while in prison, he got a few tattoos using a repurposed cassette player and melted down chess pieces, which is the toughest thing I have ever heard.) But after he became a Christian, people saw a change in him. Some of it was instant, other things were gradual, but those who were in his life saw him stop selling drugs, stop being so violent, and saw him grow in the likeness of Christ. Now, he's one of the most loving husbands and fathers I have ever seen, with a fervent love for the Word of God. While he did have a hefty past that some may discredit him for, how he lives in the present speaks volumes.

One of the best questions you can ask yourself is whether or not this thing is actually in their past or if it is just as present now, but they are good at hiding it. Some will use the passage of time as evidence of their change, but the presence of time in between incidents does not always indicate change. Have they been rehabilitated or gotten counseling? Does the pattern of their life now look different from the pattern of their life back then?

Christians live in a grace-minded reality that compels them to show grace to others. But is there a difference between showing grace and completely disregarding a sin? Justice is a very real thing – our sins may be covered in the eyes of God, but that does not mean that we won't have to pay for our sins and their ramifications in this earthly life. We need to recognize that what people did is wrong and hold them accountable while showing them grace and forgiveness. It's a delicate balancing act. Jesus was full of grace, but He was also full of truth (John 1:14). We shouldn't solely highlight one and forget about the other. Both the grace of Jesus and the truth of Jesus need to be equally appreciated and utilized.

The reality of dating is that we all have things in our past that we are not proud of. But the keyword here is "past," as in we have grown out of these things. We have gotten therapy for them, gone through rehabilitation, or done the necessary things we needed to do to not be the same person we were before Christ. There are present struggles that we need to look out for and avoid when we recognize them. If you are being physically, sexually, or emotionally abused, you need to distance yourself from the person doing those things to you. These things need to be addressed, and the person doing them to you may need to face legal action.

Discernment must be at the forefront of our minds when we consider someone's past. A person very well may have been a drug dealer at one point, which certainly is bad, but if Jesus has changed their life and they are not dealing drugs anymore (and there's a significant passage of time since their last drug deal), then I don't see why you should avoid them if the person they are in the present is a godly disciple.

But there are even more serious things from a person's past we need to mindfully discern through. For example, if someone was abusive at one point in time, then a great deal of caution needs to be used surrounding that person because you don't want to get abused yourself.[6] With a drug dealer, it is decently easy to tell if they have changed; they just needed to stop dealing drugs (I know it's often not that simple, but you hopefully understand what I am getting at). But it may be hard to see a legitimate change from that behavior with someone who was abusive. The same thing goes for someone who cheated in a relationship. If they have not had any other relationships since they cheated (or since they were abusive, in the case of the former abuser), then they have not had the chance to prove if they have been changed. It's a tough conundrum. Depending on the situation, some red flags about a person's past can simply be chalked up to immaturity, while other things tell about a person's character.

I thoroughly believe that God can change anyone from anything they once were, but I also want people to be cautious in consideration of people's past. Everyone has a past of some kind, but some things are bluntly more severe to consider. What I advise is looking at the pattern of a person's life now, consulting wise counsel, prayerfully discerning through what they did and how they are now, and not only asking them about it but people that have been in their life from then until now, if possible. It's all about discernment.

At the end of the whole evaluation process, you should be able to attest to the change in a person's life. But know that not everyone is fit to be in a romantic relationship, and you do not owe them a relationship just because they have seemingly changed. Anyone could be hiding something that you know nothing about, so it is best to always be careful. People that have done some weighty things in their past need to be mindful that people have the right to be cautious, but over time you can show the change that has happened and is happening in your life.

The grace of God in the person and work of Jesus can cover your sins, no matter what you have done. You may have to suffer the consequences for your actions in the present, but the reconciliation offered by God can cover whatever you have done.

Entitlement

A common complaint that many vocalize goes along the lines of this: "I make an effort to care for this person that I like. I've worked hard to be the best person I can be, and I treat them a lot better than the people they hang around. Why don't they like me back?" This sense of entitlement is not exclusive to Christian dating culture, as it is seen near and far and throughout various ages. People think they deserve a relationship with someone they like just for doing what they already should have been doing in the first place. Embodying things that others should probably be looking for does not mean everyone needs to notice, appreciate those things, and give you whatever you want. You might treat someone better than other people, but that doesn't mean you deserve a relationship.

Let's say that no one ever notices your godly character. Are you fine with that? Was all of it just so you could get something? It all goes back to motivation. Are you being kind and being a person of noble character because you know that is what you are supposed to be doing, or are you just doing it to get rewards for your good behavior? Lose the entitlement mindset and embrace loving others. Model the positive change you want to see, but not solely for the benefits that may come from it.

Stop Flexing, Just Follow

To detox our dating culture, we must encourage following Jesus for the sake of following Jesus and discourage the hijacking of faithfulness to be some instrument for sex appeal. We shouldn't sexualize worship, serving, or faithfulness because we want to keep our motivations pure. Flexing our faith like muscles to attract the masses to ourselves isn't what we should be aiming for. Jesus is what we should hope to see stand out from someone's life, but don't use Jesus as a wingman for you to get a guy or girl.

Am I saying we should not look for faithfulness when we are evaluating the character of someone? No, a love for God is crucial for Christians seeking to date other Christians, but each of us must ask ourselves what the reason for our faithfulness is. This is a conversation that needs to happen between you and God. Maybe bring some close friends into the discussion to ask them their motivations and have them ask you about yours. Don't overthink it, but do think it through because proper actions need proper motivations.

Discussion Questions

If you broadcast your Christianity, what is your desired outcome?

Are there things in your spiritual life that you would stop doing if you knew that no one would ever notice?

Do you have unrealistic expectations for others in terms of relationships? Have other people had unrealistic expectations for you?

What would it take for you to become convinced that someone has been changed from what they once were?

Are all people fit to be in a romantic relationship? Why or why not?

Is fame inherently wrong, or is it just how people use it?

Conclusion

Dating culture is a hodgepodge of influences, accepted practices, promoted policies, backgrounds, traditions, and expectations. With so many different factors playing a part in determining what a dating culture will look like, it can seem like a daunting task to try to change the culture. But we are not without hope, for as Professor Derik Idol says to his students, "Culture is created when one person has unshakable conviction."[1] The task of changing Christian dating culture begins with individual integrity and small-scale action before it blossoms into a larger metamorphosis.

Tagged teamed with the personal responsibility of displaying the honesty, clarity, and lack of pressure you would like to see the dating culture promote, being a person that invites having nuanced, open-minded, civil dialogue is essential. By eloquently vocalizing our hurts, concerns, suggestions, and takes, we can clarify what is impacting people the most and hopefully determine what should stay, what should go, what needs reinforcement, and what needs some adjustment.

I hope that the contents of this book have acted as a catalyst for reflection and discussion, promoting empathy and taking things to their logical end. But most of all, I hope this book inclines you to look to scripture and prompts you to prayerfully consider if you are actively helping or hurting the dating culture.

Dating is two imperfect people trying to make an imperfect relationship work by an imperfect method in an imperfect world. Relationships don't always make sense, so while I tried to give the best educated, scripturally-based guidance I could, there will always be something I did not think of or some complicated nuance I can't navigate. So while I ask you to consider my advice, I also want to highlight that results may vary. I encourage you to root yourself in the Word and wise counsel to navigate whatever unprecedented relationship situation you find yourself in.

More than likely, you disagree with me either in full or in part on some of the takes I have concluded after my observational research. You are welcome to disagree, but I encourage you to have nuanced, civil conversations about why. You could be right, I could be right, or neither of us could. But at the very least, we thought through what we are doing and why we are doing it in hopes that we will not only authentically love God but love others as well.

A deep hope I hold is that Christianity can get to a place where it makes a massive inquiring appeal to the rest of the world by standing out for its honest and healthy dating practices. After all, Christians know the greatest love of all time, so our relationships should reflect that. While not every dating relationship will or should work out, I believe that through loving one another in our practices and intents in dating, we can point to the ultimate love of the Father who sent His Son to die in our place and then raised Him from the grave.

Bonus: Miscellaneous Topics

There were some additional topics I wanted to touch on that either pertain to Christian dating or dating in general, but I did not feel as though I had enough that I wanted to say to dedicate an entire chapter to these topics. So I decided to compile them here in a miscellaneous chapter to touch on them briefly. Think of this as the proactive question and response section.

Red Flags

A notable food franchise came to a nearby town midway through my senior year of high school. We had heard of its stellar reputation in other parts of the country, so we decided to check it out for ourselves. The place was slammed because apparently, everyone had the same idea we had. As we entered, I saw a buddy of mine from across the room, so I went up and started a conversation. He was still waiting for his table, and he had been there for a while. We somehow were able to get a table due to our group's size, but after we ordered our food and drinks, we noticed that it took a very long time to get our beverages. It turns out our server had quit her job mid-shift. We looked around for the manager, and as we looked, we noticed the rampantly dirty kitchen that was plainly in view. When the manager finally arrived, he was very sweaty – not exactly what you want from the guy handling your food.

The long wait time, the way everyone looked irritated, the server quitting mid-shift, the dirty kitchen, the sort of greasy manager – these were all red flags that it was probably best if we did not eat there again. There are some prominent red flags that Christians and non-Christians should be on the lookout for because they are almost always an indication that this relationship will not be healthy for you. We will be looking at two examples for this book, but talk with your friends about other red flags that you've noticed over the years because these surely are not the only two.

Red Flag 1: if the person you are dating demands your phone password so they can read through your texts or they demand access to your social media accounts, then you probably need to leave that relationship. A relationship is built upon trust, not an aggressive dictatorship that tries to sanction who you are and are not allowed to talk to. People doing so likely have been hurt before, but being hurt in the past does not permit you to hurt somebody else in the present. There may even be the need for therapy so they can deal with why they feel the need to micromanage the entirety of your existence.

Red Flag 2: if someone who is not your spouse sends you nude pictures or asks for nude pictures, then that is a blaring red flag. Research screams that pornography (which nudes can be classified as) messes up the human brain in a variety of ways.[1] If they openly admit that they watch pornography regularly and are not fighting against it, you need to steer clear of that relationship out of respect for yourself and concern for your well-being. Unrepentant pornography use can and very well likely should be a deal-breaker for a dating relationship.

As I mentioned in an earlier chapter, the second red flag is a familiar struggle to me. I was introduced to pornography in elementary school through an episode of a late-night crime drama. Despite becoming a Christian in high school, my brain had been trained from some pivotal developmental years to be lustful, and as a result, I continue to wage war against my lust, openly admitting that I have won and lost some battles. Since sin rarely lives in a vacuum, that lustful struggle has ultimately hurt others over time, whether through a willfully wandering eye or objectification. Many of these instances occurred even after believing in Christ, which has been a weight I carry as I know I have misrepresented Christ in my actions as I wrestled with my addictions. The unfortunate exposure does not excuse or justify the behavior I take full ownership of and apologize for; that's simply a factor in the reality of what I have struggled with.

Echoing what I said in chapter seven about considering a person's past, pornography typically tries to find a way to contact you even after you have blocked its number. So when I caution you not to pursue relationships with those who actively and unrepentantly indulge in pornography, I am mindful of the fact that a person, man or woman, likely deals with the persistent symptoms of their former addiction. If they are a Christian, their sins are atoned for, and they are fully forgiven, but their sins still carry active consequences that can add hardship to their walk with Christ. The absence of active indulgence does not indicate the absence of functional effects from those past indulgences. As a result, each situation calls for grace but also critically thought through discernment. It is perfectly acceptable to discontinue or postpone a dating relationship so that you can lovingly give someone the time and space to seek restoration and healing. Their struggle may never end, but there are better places to be than others.

Having had a pornography addiction and it impacting others and knowing that pornography addictions have derailed more people than I can fathom, I can confidently say that wrestling with lust likely does not instantly disqualify anyone from future relationships (depending on the actions taken within that lust). However, perhaps a delay in a relationship should be placed until some growth out of the prominence of the addiction has taken place.

Red flags are serious, but I am genuinely convinced that God can redeem those with red flags and transform their lives to be ones that reflect His love.

Age Differences

Part of the reason why so many feel a desperate need to be either married or engaged out of college or early into their twenties is because of the way some people look at "older" people who are not in relationships. The almost instant assumption is that there is something wrong with them, or they are some sort of creep. We need to abandon the narrative that those who are single into their late 20's and beyond are the scraps leftover. This is a cultural shift that has needed implementation for a long time. While it is true that the average age of a person's first marriage has increased for both men and women, especially since the 1970's, we should not use that statistical data to make people feel like they need to dramatically lower their standards and compromise on some values just so they can be seen by society as being well along in the process of life.[2]

While he certainly can become an overused example, I doubt that many out there are looking down on the Apostle Paul for his singleness. We see from Paul's life as a single person, and we can see from Pricilla and Aquila's marriage that each can faithfully serve the Lord. There are some things that a married person can learn from their spouse that a single person cannot since they are not married, but there are also experiences and lessons a married person cannot comprehend because they are not living the same life as a single person. We each have our gifts from which we can glean experiences and wisdom. Neither singleness nor marriage should be looked down on from the viewpoint of the other.

I bring up "older" Christians because some feel uncomfortable when approached by someone five years older who is interested in going out on a date with them. Note that I am not talking about an older person approaching a minor as there are clear legal ramifications that are going on there. What I am talking about is the young adult to established adult range. I mean, should a third year in college feel weird about being asked out by a 27-year-old?

While age differences can indeed be odd if overly excessive, we need to mindfully be considerate of the value of "older" singles and how they're not clearance rack picks we should be wary of all the time. Sometimes a person may just need someone with a bit more maturity that they can't find amongst people their own age. The number of years separating two people lessens in importance as you both get older. This may solely just be a preference thing. With a significantly older spouse, there are realistic concerns about the ability to become a parent, but that's something that can be sorted through between those two people. While some relationships with drastic age differences may be weird just because they are uncommon, I don't believe there is significant biblical evidence that casts a shadow of doubt upon the relationship.

My concern lies when younger people look down on older singles, much like people did lepers in the New Testament. Some people may have just never found someone they felt like pursuing. They may have been in a long relationship that never worked out. Regardless of the reason for their singleness, increased age does not mean they are unfit to be in a relationship with.

Ladies, let's say you are 21 and a 26-year-old asks you out on a coffee date. Your initial reaction may be hesitation solely because the people around you may have convinced you that it's weird. But does that mean that you should just turn down this person solely because you have five years in between the two of you? If you liked talking with them and you found them attractive (and maybe you know some things about them, such as their proven character), then why would you let a few years get in the way of you at least seeing where things could go? You don't owe them a yes, but I feel as though it isn't too much to propose that their slightly older status not be an instant disqualifier. The same goes for older women.

For the older person asking out the younger, you need to keep in mind that you are in a different stage of life than they are. Many of your friends and people your age have probably gotten married, and you may have a heightened desire for certain "marital advantages," but you need to be mindful that the younger person, while they may have a desire to get married, is probably not as eager as you are. There is no need to rush them or yourself into a covenant just because you feel like you are missing out on something.

I hesitate to say "age is but a number" as I can easily see how that can get abused, but there is some truth behind that. We need to not look down on older singles, and for that matter, we need to not look down on singles at all. We should not treat singles like Rapunzel from Disney's Tangled, wondering when their life will begin. Their life has already started, and their life won't be made complete if they find a significant other. But, on the other side of the situation, their life won't be made lessened by finding someone. We simply need to look for the things we should be seeking in a person and not discredit or look down on those who have a few more candles on their birthday cake than us.

Unequally Yoked

Initially, I considered covering the usage of this phrase in the over spiritualization chapter, but I soon figured out that my issues with the usage of this phrase have less to do with over spiritualization and more to do with the "holier than thou" mentality that some are coming from when they use it. As I mentioned in chapter one, 2 Corinthians, where this phrase originates, bears no actual mention of marriage. But the principle that believers are not supposed to be partnered up with unbelievers, whether that means in business or marriage, can be gleaned from the phrase because of the definitively different priorities that each has.

Abuse sets in when unequally yoked is used as a tool to look down on the less mature. After all, the whole phrase is about not being unequally yoked with unbelievers, which mentions nothing of fellow believers, and yet people use the phrase as a way of saying, "I am better at being a Christian than you." If you truly are leaps and bounds further down the road in your walk with the Lord than someone else who is pursuing you, then I imagine there is a gentler way to let them down than basically saying, "I am at level 86, you're at level 3." I am not necessarily advocating for dating someone of a significantly lower spiritual maturity than you, as you want someone who will spur you on and likely need someone of similar spiritual maturity. But I just despise seeing the spiritual superiority complex card being played on people. Humility is one of the chief calls in scripture, yet acting like we can't be around others who are lesser is antithetical to this call. There are better ways of breaking up with someone than using scripture taken out of context as a boxing glove.

"The One"

Generations past and present have gotten so caught up in preferences and looking for a certain someone to come sweep them off their feet. Since its inception, Christians participating in Christian dating culture have been caught up in the concept of the One. Does God know who you will end up with if anyone? Absolutely. But does the soulmate, fairytale ending, picture-perfect One exist? There is not enough evidence to back up that it does. If one person in the line of human history married someone else's One, then the whole system collapses.

On top of that, think about people who have had spouses die and then remarried. Did they have two Ones? Realistically, the person of your dreams does not exist because, more than likely, if you imagine a dream spouse, you don't imagine their flaws.

Real human beings get acne. They fart. Their teeth and hair aren't always the nicest. They occasionally get impatient and might be rude. They inconvenience you at times. They have family and emotional baggage in some way, shape, or form. The interests you two have don't always align. Life gets busy, and they can't go to the gym as often, which results in them losing their figure. Your fantasies of the

One are just that: fantasy. If you're looking for the person of your dreams, then go to a library and read a book or go to bed and dream some more. If you're looking for an actual human being, then go out into the real world.

The concept of the One has convoluted Christian dating culture by convincing some that there is only one possible match for them in the world. But how does someone decipher if another person is this one perfect possible match? For some, they wait for some super-spiritual experience or feeling to confirm that this person is the only individual they could end up with. While some do authentically figure out that their significant other is the person they should marry through a comforting feeling deep within themselves, the lack of a spiritual feeling is not necessarily a confirmation that this is not what is destined. Our evaluation of whether someone is the person we should be with should be based on practical faith and character evaluation rather than relying on a subjective spiritual feeling.

By closing ourselves off in the name of waiting for the One and fixating on their being only one possible person for us, we isolate ourselves from the reality that there are many people we could end up with. This changes the game. We go from trying to find a needle in a haystack to there being a stack of needles. We don't have to wait for some feeling that may never come to determine if someone is this mythical perfect match. We can rely on scripture, seek wise counsel, and prayerfully consider the people around us instead of waiting for some beam of light to shine down from Heaven onto one individual.

There may be many that fit the description of what you should be looking for. Much like the concept of the multiverse, there are infinite possibilities as far as what your life could look like with any one of those persons. Make an educated, biblically-rooted decision and then seek to be faithful and thrive where you end up, not relying on spiritual butterflies in your stomach to be the chief indicator of what to do, but the truth of scripture to be your ultimate guide.

Ballin' on a Budget

In many college settings, most do not have a lot of money to splurge on. Let's say that the average person goes on 12 dates a year.

With that number in mind, it would be nearly impossible for Johnny Sophomore to go to a 5-Star restaurant every time he wanted to go on a date considering his "ramen noodles every night" budget. While I do believe in the philosophy of women being treated like princesses, that does not mean that they have to be taken out on the town with a horse-drawn carriage and a regal dinner. The standards some people have when it comes to being taken out on a date are unrealistically high and kind of egotistical.

Within Christian dating culture, I have found that some individuals idealize dates. Every little detail has to be extravagant. Picture perfect. While I am all for conjuring up a fun and unique date idea, I think Christian dating culture needs to get away from an obsession with aesthetics and everything picturesque. We need to shift our focus onto the person sitting across from us on the date and see them, flaws and all, rather than romanticizing romance. If a guy can take you on fun dates on a small budget, just imagine what he could do if he gets a full-time job. We need to stop demanding reality show dates that are carefully crafted and paid for by a team from a young adult who is probably on a meal plan or is still figuring out the basics of adulting.

Let me be clear: this does not mean you should take her to get a dollar menu hamburger if you have the budget to do more than that or to the parking lot of a local grocery store (yes, some people do that). Simply taking someone to a coffee shop and getting to know one another can be just as nice as something elaborate. A date is about what you do; it's about the person with you. With that being said, I can tell you from experience that something not working out after investing more money into the date(s) you went on hurts even worse because not only is the passenger seat of your car empty, but so is your wallet. Each situation is different. Don't be afraid to get creative and don't completely ignore the possibility of doing something nice but keep in mind that you should do something that they would actually like, not just something you are interested in. And if they are so consumeristic that they demand the whole nine yards every time, maybe that will tell you whether this is the type of person you want to be with anyway. "For richer or poorer."

Online Dating

There was a time when an American commercial break almost always consisted of at least two insurance commercials, a beer commercial, maybe an ad for a free credit report of some kind, and a commercial for an online dating service. According to a study released in early 2020, 30% of American adults said they had used a dating website or app of some kind.[3] With Christians typically not frequenting bars or nightclubs, and with some bodies of believers being full of married couples or the elderly, many young Christians find online dating to be one of the few options they have to find a significant other.

For me to provide some sort of blanket statement that all online dating is wrong would be foolish. Some beloved couples in my life (including a pastor I once had) met through a dating service or connected through social media.

The caution surrounding online dating is the same as the one surrounding regular dating: be careful. People are not always what they try to broadcast; make sure your standards are high but realistic, have a firm foundation about who you are and whose you are before getting into anything, don't put a ton of pressure on the relationship, etc.

But one large distinction to be made between online dating and regular dating is that you should be cautious about which services you use and financially support. There are upstanding people on just about every platform you can think of, but the medium through which you search for someone to date will likely tell you a lot about the kind of person you are going to encounter and what their motivations are. If you're using an app that is widely known for promoting hooking up, do you think you will find a guy or girl with a solid relationship with the Lord there? The service you use gains money from using it, so why contribute financially to something that is not promoting something biblical when there are plenty of other services out there? Be careful, just like you would anywhere else.

Is there anything wrong with a girl asking a guy out or vocalizing feelings for a guy?

The debate is ongoing as to whether or not women should initiate relationships, and the conundrum expands with every passing day. On the one hand, there appears to be evidence in scripture of the man being the one to initiate the relationship. In Proverbs 18:22, the man is the one finding his wife. Christ is the one who initiated the relationship with us, and husbands are called to give themselves up for their wives in Ephesians 5:25. Jacob worked his tail off for seven years in pursuit of Rachel (only to be duped into marrying Leah). While we recognize that it was a very different culture with very different practices back in the day, we should note the language and stories that seem to smile upon a man leading, pursuing, and initiating.

On the other hand, after countless conversations, it has come to my attention that many women feel as though they are going mad just waiting for a guy to initiate. Because of the social taboos of women asking men out on dates, many women feel like they just have to sit and twiddle their thumbs until some guy wises up. Given the desire for a man to initiate and because a lot of men would find it awkward and uncomfortable to be asked out by a woman, what is a girl to do? Is she supposed to just linger and hope that some guy strikes up the nerve to ask her out? I can only imagine how frustrating and disheartening that can become.

For some men, it might be uncomfortable to be asked out on a date by a woman. That feeling mainly stems from the fact that it is so uncommon and counter to everything we are taught growing up that it would feel unnatural. Nothing seems inherently wrong about it; it just feels off because of social taboos that are hard to grow out of. It's unusual and therefore uncomfortable, but just because it is uncomfortable does not mean it is instantly wrong. But for me, and I believe for many others, a woman telling me that she is interested in going out does not seem awkward; it feels honest and clear. Just like how when a guy asks a girl out, it is up to her whether or not she says yes. When a girl tells a guy that she likes him, the ball is then placed into his court on whether he will take the initiative to ask her out on a date. There is communication, vulnerability, and opportunity for the man to initiate in this situation, but from an informed standpoint. You don't have to like the other person at the level they like you for you to go out on a date. Just take it slow, be casual but intentional, and have a good time.

I believe there is some biblical backing to this approach found in the book of Ruth. After noticing the steadfast character of Boaz and how he cared for her when she was in his field, Ruth listened to the instruction of Naomi and laid at the feet of Boaz while he was sleeping. "...I am Ruth, your servant. Spread your wings over your servant, for you are a redeemer."[4] She let him know that she wanted him, and then the ball was in his court to either take it or leave it. Thankfully, he takes initiative and makes the necessary cultural arrangements to have her as his own. Perhaps this is reading too much of my modern context into the biblical text, but I am purely looking at patterns and don't see an outright condemnation of women initiating relationships with men.

Although Ruth and Boaz had known each other for a brief amount of time, there was at least some history between the two. But what about if we see someone for the first time? To say that having a stranger, girl or guy, come up to you and confess their love for you would be creepy is an understatement. For girls, I would say that if you want a guy to ask you out in that particular situation, then maybe you can be bold and just give a guy your number. The ball is then in his court to either take the initiative to ask you out or not. Or perhaps you can just go over and introduce yourself – he will likely ask if he is interested. Lastly, maybe sit apart from your group of friends within sight of the guy. Few things are more socially intimidating than a pack of girls altogether because if a guy were to come up to try to talk to you, he not only has to face you but your friends as well.

Guys: I know that it is scary and heart racing to walk up to a girl you do not know and ask her out on a date, but I am willing to bet that there is little to no chance of her laughing in your face if you try. I am not guaranteeing that she will say yes, and you need to not pressure her to say yes, but a lot of girls take it as a compliment that a guy would be so bold as to ask them out on a date without any prior knowledge as to what they are like. Make sure you use the word date when you ask. Take initiative, have no expectations, be kind, and try not to take it personally if she says no. Just because you have boldness does not mean that you are entitled to a yes for a date.

The Enneagram and a "Reality" Show

It seems like no one asks for people's numbers anymore. Actually, I take that back; people are still asking for other people's numbers, but it's not phone numbers anymore; it's Enneagram numbers. From books to podcasts to hour-long conversations aimed at people trying to discover more about themselves, the Enneagram and other personality tests like it are everywhere and impact the way we interact. There have been times when my knowledge of someone's alleged Enneagram type has helped me approach them in the most loving way I can. But in regards to dating, the Enneagram has added a vague and tricky layer to the complexity.

"But what if he's a ___ and I am a ___" is a common thing you will hear due to people thinking that because they have a little bit of a potential personality conflict, then that must mean that the relationship they might have is destined to fall apart or be miserable. When I hear people writing someone off based on the Enneagram, I can't help but laugh a little as I jokingly think that arranged marriages might not be such a bad idea. While I am sure there are many horror stories to choose from in regards to arranged marriages, there is a sort of allure to the idea of just getting into something significant and making it work without all the hustle and preoccupation with things like Enneagram number compatibility and whether or not he or she has a pleasing social media aesthetic.

Nowadays, if we don't like something for whatever reason, there are at least five different alternative options for what you were looking for. Don't like a streaming service? There are eight more to choose from. Searching for a type of headphones but don't want to pay a lofty amount for the real thing? Go off-brand and venture into some alternative headphones. We are bombarded with options and are trained for instant gratification, resulting in a recoiling and fleeing phenomenon the second something does not match up to our expectations or does not work the way we think it should.

The only other pop culture influence that debatably matches up to the Enneagram in terms of impact and influence is a particular popular reality TV show. Thirty beautiful eligible women from a variety of backgrounds and career paths are brought to a gorgeous mansion where they meet, flirt with, and try to secure the affections of a single eligible man, with different female contestants being sent home every week as the man determines whether or not he senses a connection with them based off their one-on-one dates or group interactions. Dramatic? You bet. Entertaining? At times. It is more infuriating than anything else. But there is an addictive quality to the show thanks to its drama, poor decision-making, betrayal, and unpredictability at times. In full confession, I've even jokingly applied for the show myself.

Arguably the most infuriating aspect of the show is how it seems like contestants have to be always on and nearly perfect to move on each week, and even then, it does not seem like that is enough sometimes. I think that the vast amount of people out there can effectively determine what they should copy from what they see on TV and what they should not copy into their own life, but at times we see people adopting this "one strike, you're out" mindset.

People start discontinuing relationships because the guy forgot to open a door one time or because a girl had never seen a film franchise. Oddly, pettiness infiltrates our dating lives at the influence of TV shows like this one. It is often subtle, but some people can't differentiate between real life and the producer and viewer-influenced, edited romance we see on screen.

There is entertainment that can be found in reality TV, and there are things we can learn using the Enneagram, but when we rely too heavily on those things and let their toxic aspects influence our dating lives, we become petty over-spiritualized fools. Take a step back and assess whether or not you are letting the things of this world influence you, whether it be personality tests or entertainment, and get your mind renewed by adhering to the Word of God as Paul talks about in Romans 12.[5]

MRS Degree

Have you ever been to Buc-ee's? You would know if you have been and if you haven't, you're missing out. It's a gas station/convenience store mainly located in Texas. I've been to my fair share of gas stations and convenience stores in my lifetime. I thought I knew what the epitome of a gas station/convenience store was supposed to look like, but when I walked into Buc-ee's for the first time, I realized I was sorely mistaken. The store just goes on and on. I lost a pound by the time I walked from one end of the store to the next. There's clothing, games, neck pillows, food, groceries. You name it, they probably have it. If I take a girl to Buc-ee's, just know that I am very serious about that girl, as I consider Buc-ee's a great location for a date. There was just more at Buc-ee's than I had ever seen before.

That feeling I felt when I walked into Buc-ee's for the first time is what I imagine many people feel when they walk on a college campus for the first time – you've never seen so many options. College is full of options, and people know it. Some people go to college solely for the options. Some people go to college, paying all that money, going through all the forms and campus tours, all the scholarship hunts, with the primary motivation for their attendance being finding a spouse. These people are cleverly referred to as MRS or MR majors (typically, I see this being a more common practice for females than males, so I will be referring only to MRS degrees throughout this section, but it encapsulates both circumstances). I've heard tales of parents being the primary encouragers of it. Some schools have even used the fact that students may find their spouse while at their college as a magnetic admission recruiting tool.[6]

Is anything wrong with finding a spouse? No. Is there a problem with going to college for the sole purpose of finding a spouse without an ounce of care about your education? Possibly. I'll attempt to explain why. First and foremost, we are not promised spouses, marriage, kids, or anything like that, even though there is the command to be fruitful and multiply.[7] As Paul says in 1 Corinthians 7:6-7, "Now as a concession, not a command, I say this. I wish that all were as I myself am. But each has his own gift from God, one of one kind and one of another." Paul actually encourages singleness. He doesn't encourage you to flee from it desperately. The MRS degree mentality typically closes its mind completely off to the possibility that God's will could be taking you in a different direction.

If God didn't answer your prayers for a spouse, would you still follow Him? You may have an unhealthy obsession with marriage if you invested thousands into college, not really for education but rather just to find a spouse. If you were that fixated on finding a spouse, why not just pay for an online dating service instead of a significantly more expensive college degree? If a person's primary motivation behind every connection they make is "I have to find my spouse ASAP," then they are virtually eliminating any possibility of just ordinary friendship, which is a perfectly good thing to have.

Four core questions need to be asked and answered honestly by those pursuing an MRS degree: are you even interested in the academic degree you are pursuing, do you even intend on using it ever? Why do you feel like you need to find a spouse in college? What are you going to do if you don't find a spouse in college?

College isn't cheap and while some people choose to give up careers and not use that degree as they originally intended because they want to focus on raising a family, going into college with no interest in what you are academically pursuing is unwise stewardship of your time, scholarships, and other resources. Since you're not guaranteed a spouse in college or any time in life, take what you are studying in college seriously and go into a field you are passionate about.

In his book *Just Do Something,* Kevin DeYoung explains his position that perhaps there are many women out there who would rather start a family than a career, but because no man has taken the initiative with marriage, they feel as though they need to pursue a degree that is not where their heart is.[8] I see and hear this point. In specific circumstances, I would say that maybe it would be wiser to forgo or abandon the pursuit of an educational degree in pursuit of marriage. But I would caution that just because we desire to be married, that does not mean that we will any time soon or ever. Therefore, it is generally wiser to focus your energy on your career rather than just fixating on getting a spouse. You can get a spouse anywhere, but you can only get a degree in school.

A lot of the intent behind the pursuit of an MRS degree comes from people planning out their futures. We get so caught up in the idea of being a wife or husband, a mother or father, or whatever else that we ignore the possibility that maybe God has other plans. When I started looking at colleges, I wanted to be a theatre major. By the time I applied, I wanted to be a youth pastor. Once I got to college, I went for a Project Management degree with minors in youth ministry and creative writing. The plans that I originally had for myself changed vastly, especially when I opened up to the possibility that God had other plans for what my life was going to look like.

Life's not linear, but when we try to control everything, we act as if it is. Don't hold onto your thought-out future so much that you never allow for things to be shaken up. It's great to set goals, but hold your goals and plans loosely because God may have other ideas. Whatever His plans are, you are called to faithfulness wherever you end up and in whatever you are doing, single or not, college graduate or not.

Interracial Relationships

Emmett Till was just 14 years old when he was murdered in Mississippi in 1955. He was beaten to the point where he was so disfigured that the only way someone could have identified his body was by looking at the initialed ring he wore. He was shot, tied to a heavy object using barbed wire, and drowned because he allegedly whistled at a white woman. Emmett's mother held an open casket funeral viewing so that the world could see what the two racists who killed him had done to her boy. The photographs are horrific, but what is also horrific is that the vile hatred we see exhibited in the case of Emmett Till still lives on today.

The idea of a person of color being with a white person disgusts some people, whether they will openly say it or not. Over the years, as I have encountered more people with a negative view of interracial relationships, I have asked where that view comes from and why they hold to it. The answers have varied from "that's just how I was raised" to misinterpretations of Biblical passages. Using the "you can't teach an old dog new tricks" philosophy to defend your racial prejudices instead of thoughtfully dealing with them signals laziness in sanctification and growth. We must never stop learning and growing, so the notion that you always have to adhere to how you were raised is nonsense. Furthermore, God is not against interracial relationships, as we will discuss in this section. The misinterpretation of scripture and the neglect to observe its proper context to defend your racism is not pleasing to God, who triumphantly delights in interracial relationships.

Let's start by pointing out that we are all created in the image of God.[9] From the very bones and veins beneath our skin to the hairs on our head, we are crafted by our Creator—every last one of us. Jesus lived on Earth as a first-century Jew (not as a pale white man, as some portraits try to indicate) who lived in areas such as Bethlehem and Egypt. The devaluing of other races appalled our Savior. After all, Christ came from a genealogy that contained both Jews and Gentiles. Christ associated commonly with Gentiles from the Roman Centurion who He said had remarkable faith that He had not found in Israel to the Samaritan woman at the well.[10] Jesus even told the parable of the Good Samaritan, which has implications that kick racism in its ugly teeth. Christ valued races other than His own. Other races mattered to Christ because His Father had created them all in His image, so therefore they should matter to us just as they do to Him.

Those in opposition to interracial relationships commonly cite Deuteronomy 7 verse 3: "You shall not intermarry with them, giving your daughters to their sons or taking their daughters for your sons," but the reason God commands that is because of what is said in verse 4, "…for they would turn away your sons from following me, to serve other gods. Then the anger of the Lord would be kindled against you, and he would destroy you quickly." The passage is about the protection of religious purity, not some sort of "racial purity." This command to not intermarry with another group was specific to this scenario, not prescriptive for us today. It is prescriptive to us in the sense of not marrying people who are not of the same faith, but not in the sense of not intermarrying with other tribes or nations.

Let us not assume that God just passively sits on His throne and complains to His angels that racism is happening. In Numbers 12, where Miriam and Aaron confronted Moses about the fact that he had married a Cushite woman, the text seems to indicate that they were possibly confronting Moses because of the opposition they had to his marriage with a woman from a different nation. God then gave Miriam leprosy and forced her to live outside of the camp of the Israelites for a week.

In Revelation 7:9-10, a great multitude is standing before the throne with people from every nation, tribe, and tongue in attendance. They are all crying out, "Salvation belongs to our God who sits on the throne, and to the Lamb!" God is evidently fine with interracial relationships and made it a point to tell us that there would be all races congregated in Heaven, praising their mutual God and King. There will be products of interracial relationships in Heaven. Scripture does not disagree with interracial relationships.

A 2005 sermon by John Piper told the story of Warren Webster, a former missionary to Pakistan, who was asked what he would do if his daughter wanted to marry a Pakistani boy she met while on the mission field. "With great forcefulness, [Webster] said: 'The Bible would say, better a Christian Pakistani than a godless white American!'"[11] God is sovereignly concerned about the pairing of believers and unbelievers, but lost no rest on the seventh day over whether two people of different races started a relationship together.

However, just because God is fine with your interracial relationship, that does not mean His Creation will be. Interracial couples will likely have to walk through some issues that couples of the same race likely will never have to go through due to some people's ignorance, prejudice, and racism. This calls for patience and open ears from both parties in the relationship but a strong commitment to loving one another enough to stand up in gentleness for one another. Your mind should be fixated on the fact that both the oppressed and the oppressor are made in the image of God. Although we should not enable racism, we should be loving enough to approach people in gentleness to seek reconciliation as a witness to God's grace for both the oppressed and the oppressors.

For those of us not in interracial relationships, we should keep those that are in our prayers in light of the things they have to deal with. We need to stand by them and be there for them. We need to ask for God's searching of our hearts and ask that he lead us in the way everlasting as we identify the grievous ways in ourselves.[12]

Discussion Questions

If there is a topic I did not cover that you wish I had, what is it? Who are some trusted friends you would like to engage with in that conversation?

Has your stance on any particular matter changed after reading this book? If so, what and why?

What are some instant red flags you can identify in terms of relationships?

Would you date someone older or younger than you (so long as it's legal)? What do you think would be some of the things you would have to navigate?

If you started going on dates with someone, who are the people you feel like you would have to tell from the beginning?

In your opinion, does "the One" exist?

What are some fair expectations for a first date?

Have you ever ghosted or been ghosted by someone? If you have done it, what was your reason for doing so?

Would you consider participating in a dating app or online dating service? Why or why not?

Is there anything wrong with a girl asking a guy out or vocalizing feelings for a guy?

If there is a topic I did not cover that you wish I had, what is it? Who are some trusted friends you would like to engage with in that conversation?

Has your stance on any particular matter changed after reading this book? If so, what and why?

Notes
A Quick Distinction: "Christian"

1. Foreman, Jon. "Another Switchfoot Concert." Interview by Tim Challies. Blog post. *Tim Challies*. 10 July 2004. Web. 26 Aug. 2021.

Coffeehouse, John Oliver, and Surveys

1. Crawford, Natalie. "Every Girl Has a Liberty Boy Horror Story Ladies I Wanna Know Yours." *Twitter*. Twitter, 24 Feb. 2020. Web. 26 Aug. 2021.

Should Christians Only Date Other Christians?

1. The ramifications of the disobedience that Israelites had towards God's commands is felt in the book of Judges. Many of the Israelites during that time likely felt as though they could be a positive influence in the life of unbelievers but as we see in Judges, the influence seemed to work the other way around.

2. Romans 10:17

3. There is some nuance to be had with this particular conversation. The circumstances around a romantic relationship vary incredibly, so it is virtually impossible to encapsulate and address all the unique situations that could come up between a believer and an unbeliever. I met a man recently who became a Christian during his relationship to someone who was not a believer. He did not break up with her instantly the second that he became a Christian. Instead, he tried to invite her to consider the Gospel, but she rejected Christianity and eventually him. I feel as though he did right based on his specific situation, but could also see the point being made by those who would say he should have broken up with her soon after becoming a Christian. There are some general principles to follow, but with the

unique nature of relationships, things are rarely spelled out. More than likely, some prayerful, scripture-saturated navigation will need to take place.

4. Thompson Day, Heather. "My Dad (a Pastor) Took Me on a Drive in College & Said 'Never date a Man for His Potential. Make Your Decisions Based off Who He Is Right Now Assuming Nothing Will Change' There Are Bad Ppl in Religion But There Are Also Really beautiful Ppl, & We Must Tell Both STORIES." *Twitter*. Twitter, 26 Dec. 2019. Web. 26 Aug. 2021.

5. Mark 4:8

6. Proverbs 30:31, Titus 3:5

7. Isaiah 55:8-9

8. 1 Corinthians 7:12-13

9. Hosea 1:2

10. *Chad Poe - Liberty University Convocation. YouTube.* Liberty University, 07 Mar. 2019. Web. 26 Aug. 2021.

11. Hosea 3:2. God isn't opposed to oatmeal raisin cookies if that is all you focused on in that verse.

12. Brown, Allan P. "Did God Command Hosea to Marry A Harlot?" *God's Bible School & College*. 20 Sept. 2018. Web. 26 Aug. 2021.

13. Hindson, Edward E., and Gary E. Yates. "Hosea." *The Essence of the Old TESTAMENT: A Survey*. Nashville, TN: B & H Academic, 2012. 372. Print.

14. Sprinkle, Preston M. *Charis: God's Scandalous Grace for Us*. Colorado Springs, CO: David C Cook, 2014. ~~105. Print.~~

15. Yes, we should show abundant grace. But no, we should not seek out and marry an active prostitute. This in no way indicates that prostitutes cannot be desirable or carry no worth, rather this guidance is for the purpose of remaining faithful.

16. Isaiah 20:1-3, Ezekiel 5:1-4, Ezekiel 4:15

17. Revelation 19:7–9, 21:1-2

Under pressure

1. Rabin, Roni Caryn. "Put a Ring on It? Millennial Couples Are in No Hurry." *The New York Times*. 29 May 2018. Web. 26 Aug. 2021.

2. Genesis 1:28

3. Ephesians 6:4, Proverbs 29:15, Deuteronomy 6:6-9, among others

4. 1 Timothy 1:2

5. "Foster Care Numbers up for Fifth Straight Year." *The North American Council on Adoptable Children (NACAC)*. 16 Apr. 2021. Web. 26 Aug. 2021.

6. Ephesians 1:3-14

7. 2 Timothy 4:21, Romans 16:13, 23, Colossians 14:15

8. Psalm 16:11

9. These questions are a mixture of common knowledge questions I came up with or was inspired by from Clayton

and Sharie King's "12 Questions to Ask Before You Marry" and Timothy Keller's "The Meaning of Marriage."

10. Proverbs 18:22

Over spiritualization

1. *597. Should Christians Say, "God Told Me..."?* Dir. Bobby Conway. *YouTube*. One Minute Apologist, 22 Oct. 2014. Web. 26 Aug. 2021.

2. Greear, J. D. *Jesus, Continued...: Why the SPIRIT inside You Is Better than JESUS beside You*. Grand Rapids, MI: Zondervan, 2014. 112-13. Print.

3. DeYoung, Kevin. *Just Do Something: A Liberating Approach to Finding God's Will*. Chicago: Moody, 2014. 82-83. Print.

4. 1 Corinthians 7:34

5. Keep in mind that there are vast differences between going on a few dates and a breakup, so the explanation's depth may not need to be as thorough for ending things after a few dates as it would for a long term "official" relationship. If you've just gone on a date or two, a simple "I just don't want to continue things" is clear enough and takes personal ownership, but a half a year relationship may need an elaboration on your reasons if you can articulate them.

6. Brown, Paige Benton. "Singled Out for Good." *ReGeneration Quarterly,* 1997. Print. The article is posted numerous places online, including River Rock Bible. You should be able to find it with a simple search online.

7. Philippians 4:11-13, Proverbs 3:5

Want a Word? Read the Word

1. Proverbs 9:10

2. Mark 12:30-31

3. Proverbs 31, 1 Timothy 3

4. Proverbs 11:14, 19:20

5. Ruth 1:14-22

6. Ruth 2:15-16

7. Ruth 2:8-9

8. Piper, John. "A Metaphor of Christ and the Church." *Desiring God.* 12 Feb. 1984. Web. 26 Aug. 2021.

9. Keller, Timothy, and Kathy Keller. *The Meaning of Marriage: Facing the Complexities of Commitment with the Wisdom of God.* New York, NY: Penguin, 2016. 133. Print.

10. *Fantasy Girl | Jonathan "JP" Pokluda - Oct. 23, 2018.* Jonathan Pokluda. *YouTube.* The Porch, 11 Nov. 2018. Web. 26 Aug. 2021.

11. 1 Corinthians 7:6-7

12. 1 Corinthians 7:28, Ephesians 5:25-33, Ecclesiastes 4:12

13. Revelation 1:8

14. Psalm 139:23-24

The Motivation Rarely Admitted

1. Isom, Mo. *Sex, Jesus, and the Conversations the Church Forgot.* Grand Rapids: Baker Group, 2018. 47-48. Print.

2. 1 Corinthians 7:8-9

3. Yuan, Christopher. *Holy Sexuality and the Gospel: Sex, Desire, and Relationships Shaped by God's Grand Story.* Multnomah, 2018. 117. Print.

4. *Staying In Love | David Marvin. YouTube.* The Porch, 25 Oct. 2019. Web. 26 Aug. 2021.

5. Sex is a hard topic to discuss because there are virtually infinite layers and subtopics within the broader topic. My apologies if I did not specifically address an aspect of the sex conversation within this chapter, but I wrote about what I felt comfortable in writing and trust that other conversations (such as sexual baggage, healing from the deep wounds of purity culture, etc.) are better handled by other authors or even a therapist. At the very least, I hope that my writings on the topic will ignite conversations that can include some of the topics I did not discuss.

Flexing Faith

1. Romans 5:8

2. *Philippians 1:15-18*

3. Vinopal, Lauren. "A Year-by-year Guide to Your Risk of Divorce." *Fatherly.* 05 Aug. 2021. Web. 26 Aug. 2021.

4. Keller, Timothy, and Kathy Keller. *The Meaning of Marriage: Facing the Complexities of Commitment with the Wisdom of God.* New York, NY: Penguin, 2016. 89. Print.

5. Keller, Timothy, and Kathy Keller. *The Meaning of Marriage: Facing the Complexities of Commitment with the Wisdom of God.* New York, NY: Penguin, 2016. 132. Print.

6. Note that I am referring to emotional abuse, not sexual or physical abuse. From my understanding, a practice like gaslighting, for example, though emotionally abusive, can be grown out of. Even though someone can grow out of their former practices of emotional abuse, the consequences of that abuse are still real and impact people's lives. Their emotional abuse was not justified, but it's possible to recognize one's past tactics and maturely change. Sexual and physical abuse, however, are not things to be chalked up to childish immaturity. In no way am I advocating for getting into a relationship with someone who domestically assaulted their past significant other or sexually assaulted someone else just because it has been a few years. These are examples of past behaviors and actions that are way more significant in impact and very well may disqualify someone from a romantic relationship. My point in this section still stands that people can be changed by God and pasts need to be considered and navigated, but I do not want this section to be distorted as some allowance or justification of sexual or physical abuse.

Conclusion

1. Idol, Derik. "Building a Culture." YOUT 220: Global Youth Culture Class. Liberty University, Lynchburg, VA. 2019. Lecture.

Bonus: Miscellaneous Topics

1. Ghose, Tia. "Bye, Bye, Playboy Bunnies: 5 Ways Porn Affects the Brain." *LiveScience*. 13 Oct. 2015. Web. 26 Aug. 2021.

2. "Historical Marital Status Tables." *The United States Census Bureau*. 23 Nov. 2020. Web. 26 Aug. 2021.

3. Anderson, Monica, Emily A. Vogels, and Erica Turner. *The Virtues and Downsides of Online Dating*. Rep. Pew Research, 6 Feb. 2020. Web. 26 Aug. 2021.

4. Ruth 3:9

5. This section should not be read as a promotion or approval of the Enneagram, as I am cautious about its usage due to its origins, which you can hear more about by listening to Cultish's podcast episodes on the topic or by reading "Richard Rohr and the Enneagram Secret" by Don and Joy Veinot and Martia Montenegro.

6. Desrets, Christa. "Liberty's Marriage Proposal." *The News & Advance*. 10 May 2009. Web. 26 Aug. 2021.

7. Genesis 1:28

8. DeYoung, Kevin. *Just Do Something: A Liberating Approach to Finding God's Will*. Chicago: Moody, 2014. 108-09. Print.

9. Genesis 1:26

10. Matthew 9:10, John 4

11. Piper, John. "Racial Harmony and Interracial Marriage." *Desiring God*. 16 Jan. 2005. Web. 26 Aug. 2021.

12. Psalm 139:24

Acknowledgements

My Family: Being able to run things by trusted sources who have my best interest at heart was crucial to the development of this project. I count myself blessed to be born a Swain.

Emlee Sanderford: Over the course of this project I received vast amounts of encouragement, inquiry, and support from scores of people but few have been as adamant as you, to the point where you edited my book. I recommend Emlee for any and all projects.

Jim Peper: I'm forever grateful for Brandi introducing us and for the constant friend, resource, mentor, and confidant you have been over the years, even though we are states away.

Tyler Cash: Sasha and the boys are lucky to have you, and many are blessed by your impact.

Madelyn Mauck: Your initial logo design for my social media accounts gave a face to the project and motivated me to see the rest of it come together.

The Wilson Avenue Gospel Community Group: One of the hardest parts of moving away for a new job was knowing that I was not going to be sitting in the Foster's living room every Thursday night. You encouraged, loved, and spiritually challenged me in the best of ways.

Derik Idol, The Leighs, Tatum Sheppard, Walker Sandler: You all were a resource to me and I cannot thank you enough for your viewpoint, your encouragement, and your listening ear.

Izzi Diaz, Draya Quiambao, and Kiersten Wilder: Getting to run so many things by you was invaluable for this book. Also, thank you for your vast appreciation for Pride & Prejudice.

Student Activities: Thank you for the platform to practice my writing, for eventually inspiring this book, and for being the best job a college student could have. I could not imagine my college experience without the friendships and memories I made at my job. You are all "game changers."

Consider Supporting Landen In Ministry

Over the course of writing this book, I realized that our core commissioning is not for the good gift of marriage, but rather for making disciples (Matthew 28:16-20). Convicted by the Great Commission, I applied to work with Young Life, a parachurch youth ministry dedicated to reaching people with the Gospel. After being hired, I moved to the Bucks County, PA area to begin investing into the lives of teens, trying to earn the right to be heard, showing and sharing with them the good news of Jesus, and inviting them to leverage their teenage years for the Kingdom.

Ministries like this take a village to operate, and so while I do ask that you add Bucks County Young Life to your prayer list, I also want to invite you to steward the resources God has blessed you with by partnering with our area financially. Whether one-time, yearly, or monthly, your contribution to our area will help bring the Gospel to teenagers in the Philadelphia area. Additionally, I encourage you to do research into your own area to see if you can partner with your local Young Life team. If you do choose to donate, I would love to thank you personally.

To donate directly to Landen Swain's Young Life efforts in Bucks County, use this link:

https://giving.younglife.org/landenswain

(The inclusion of these links does not denote that the organization of Young Life funds, supports, or promotes this book.)

If you would like to book Landen for your conference, convocation, chapel, podcast, or gathering, you can contact him at landenswain.com

Consider following @DetoxChristianDating on Instagram and TikTok

Made in the USA
Middletown, DE
14 October 2021